MARKETING IN EMERGING COMPANIES

Marketing in Emerging Companies

Robert T. Davis

Stanford University   Graduate School of Business

F. Gordon Smith

World Trade in Computers, Inc.

ADDISON-WESLEY PUBLISHING COMPANY

Reading, Massachusetts ▪ Menlo Park, California
Wokingham, Berkshire ▪ Amsterdam ▪ Don Mills, Ontario ▪ Sydney

Library of Congress Cataloging in Publication Data

Davis, Robert Tyrrell.
  Marketing in emerging companies.

  Includes index.
  1. Marketing. I. Smith, F. Gordon. II. Title.
  HF5415.D375 1984   658.8   84-11006
  ISBN 0–201–10377–X

Cover design by Marshall Henrichs
Text design adapted from one by The Cambridge Studio
Set in 10 point Melior by Grafacon, Inc.

ISBN 0–201–10377–X

ABCDEFGHIJ–AL–8654

Contents

Preface

After surviving the often long climb to sustained profitability, it is not unusual for the management teams of many emerging companies to pause and reflect. The period of reflection often leads to an attempt to rationalize the business, primarily in terms of products sold and of markets served. Done well, this rationalization process inevitably leads to marketing, the subject of this important book.

Why marketing? Why not production or finance or technology? The answer is straightforward and twofold. First, in smartly run businesses today, the traditional functions are beginning to overlap. Second, marketing, broadly defined, serves as an interface between the business enterprise and the rapidly changing outside world. To subordinate this activity in linear times is dangerous for a high rise company. To do so in exponential times is likely to be fatal. One does not have to read many issues of *Business Week*, *Fortune*, or the *Wall Street Journal* to verify this peril.

The response to the challenge and threat of the times has been dramatic. it is now fashionable to be "market-driven" and "customer-oriented." The world is suddenly awash with marketeers. But talk and buzz words are cheap . . . and plentiful. The real thing—a truly marketing-sensitive management team and style—is still relatively hard to come by. And it is the real thing that will separate the winners from the mere players among the crop of companies growing up in the 1980's.

Many new modes of thinking on just what true marketing sensitivity is all about are flowing both from academia and from the real world of practice. Bob Davis and Gordon Smith have positioned their book squarely at the intersection of these two spheres. The days of practitioners scoffing at professors and vice versa are past. Both schools—hard knocks and the chalkboard variety—will continue to make complementary contributions to the advance of business management. Reality is the father of mutual respect.

In the pages that follow is knowledge distilled from thoughtful pondering, trial and error, successes and failures. It has been used with services and products in industrial and consumer markets. The finished material has stood the rugged test of classroom exposure before hundreds of practicing, critical executives from all walks of business. This book is destined to become the handy guide to modern, pragmatic marketing for the management teams of companies on the move.

Steven C. Brandt

Stanford University
Graduate School of Business

Introduction

Probably the most recurring temptation for new management is to buy into the enticing belief that good products sell themselves. After all, customers are sensible and recognize the value of new ideas! Well, maybe they do and maybe they don't. Scores of companies are launched with the fervent hope that a new technology, a product breakthrough, or an intriguing service idea will suffice to produce untold wealth. And scores of disappointed managers find out too late that the product didn't quite fit, that the buyers were boorishly uninterested, that the channels were already preempted, that the competition was more imaginative than presumed.

Marketing may not automatically solve all of these problems, but without it the chances of business success are severely limited. The marketing issues are typically the "make or break" decisions for the new enterprise. It makes sense, therefore, to focus this book upon the senior management of emerging enterprises who haven't yet cast their plans in concrete. Most of these executives are not marketing specialists. They grew up in finance, engineering, research, or sales. So it becomes pertinent to ask: what do they have to know about marketing? What skills should they look for in their marketing manager? What can they reasonably expect from this activity? And then, from the point of view of the marketing manager, how should he or she carry out the position? What marketing ideas are likely to prove most beneficial?

The emerging company is an inviting subject. It normally starts with a clean slate and, it is hoped, with a viable idea. It has no history, and its future success is very much in the hands of the present management team. Although prospects and hopes are high, the competitive threat is serious. Resources are limited, and somehow management must thread its course between the extremes of bare-bones operations and an experienced staff of resident experts. In most start-ups, needless to say, "bare bones" is the only alternative, and there is little, if any, room for error. Resources must be concentrated and action centered on the significant decision areas. The marketing issues to be decided are basic, and their impact is highly leveraged. Thus, it is imperative that management in these emerging companies understand the potentials, as well as the limitations, of marketing. Because the essential function of the business is to create satisfied customers, marketing stands out as the functional kingpin. This doesn't mean, of course, that R&D, engineering, manufacturing, and finance are not vital—rather that the world of customers is the direct responsibility of the activity called marketing. Marketing is therefore the controller. At the same time, all the business functions are integral parts of an overall management system.

To underscore this point, management decisions involving new products and markets require positive answers to three questions:

1. Are the product and the market viable?

2. Can we do it?

3. Will the payoff be worthwhile?

There are many subquestions to each of these, but the three represent the foundation for all business growth decisions. It is clear that the implications of the three questions are profound and affect every facet of the company, be it research, engineering, manufacturing, or marketing.

The marketing manager, however, is particularly sensitive since his or her charge is to identify and realize market opportunities. The answers to the three questions become the marketing manager's checklist for a go, no-go entry decision. The three questions, it follows, underlie all of the material in this book; they are the ever-present decision criteria.

The content of this book represents our accumulated experience over thirty years, in the business world for one of us and in the academic world for the other. We hope that the mix will provide a useful offering to the management of "take-off" companies. We have tried to be aware of the multidimensioned real world by using examples from all kinds of companies and industries. We do have a bias, owing to our backgrounds, for direct-selling "equipment" type of situations, but we hope that the concepts will nonetheless be applicable in most situations.

We owe thanks to a number of people who either provided information or were willing to read various parts of the manuscript. These included Jack Warne, Jim Morrell, Red Scott, and Alan Nichols.

Our special thanks go to Alyce Adams, who not only suffered through the ordeal of typing four or five drafts, but also took the time to read the material and check it for consistency and clarity.

MARKETING IN EMERGING COMPANIES

1

Some Definitions

WHAT IS MARKETING?

We have elected to define business marketing four ways, each of which contributes its own useful perspective. The imaginative reader might well lengthen the list, but the four that are discussed capture well the essential dimensions of the subject.

Definition 1: Specialty versus Commodity

Marketing represents those efforts by management to maintain a specialty position in the marketplace. It is reasonable to assume that most business people prefer to run their companies from a specialty position, the opposite being commodity. The extremes can be easily diagramed on a simple continuum:

Specialty ⟶ Commodity

This continuum is usually referred to as the *product (or service) life cycle* and is depicted as a curve:

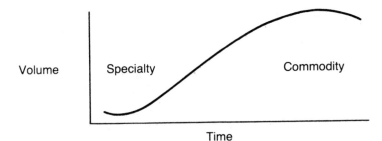

The ultimate specialty is a monopoly, hopefully habit-forming. Uniqueness is its distinguishing characteristic. At the opposite pole there is the commodity world, which exists whenever management's offer to its customers is identical with its competitor's offer.

A moment's reflection reinforces the notion that the commodity definition is a bit tricky. What is the offer? Quite clearly it starts with the physical product or specific service—the microcomputer or the coach seat to New York. But the consumer almost always makes the buying decision on the basis of additional values—the seller's reputation, some personal relationships, the delivery schedule, the product's availability, or the back-up service. These are all ingredients of the seller's offer, and are usually dissimilar among competitors. Hence, it is fair to say that pure commodity markets are rare. This doesn't mean, by the same token, that all of these differentiating variables are equally important to all of the buyers; nor that one, most commonly price, won't outweigh the others. Nevertheless, it would be an expensive mistake to ignore the fact that some types of buyers have different preferences than others and that the product's optimal mix of values will vary by segment.

We normally associate commodity marketing with raw materials. After all, economists have traditionally used the commodity exchanges as their models of perfect competition on the assumption that the products are not differentiated. And yet it is conceivable to have commodity-like markets even when technology is complex. This coexistence of technology with commodity seems a contradiction in terms, to be sure, but what about the semiconductor industry? It is hard to imagine any more complicated technology, and yet the participants operate much as if they were dealing in "undifferentiated goods." In point of fact, the semiconductor business comes close to meeting the economist's definition of perfect competition: so many buyers and sellers that no one buyer or seller has any particular impact upon the market; the market sets the price; lead times are discussed in matters of weeks and months (not years); and knowledge is widespread and generally available to all. One look at the advertising pages of the personal computing magazines is convincing evidence of hundreds of emerging companies trying to avoid the commodity classification.

A specialty business has one meaningful advantage over a commodity business—competition is not based exclusively on price. Indeed, it makes little sense for the specialty business to cut price against itself. On the other hand, it can't set any price it wants because at some point it would price the product right out of the market. For most products there is an eventual substitute. But the fact remains that the specialist has a great deal of pricing freedom.

For the commodity house, on the other hand, price is the only competitive weapon. By definition prices must be the same. If, in a particular case, there is some degree of price differentiation, then the competitor may be pushing the commodity extreme, but is not fully there.

Specialty marketing has several presumed advantages. The business is likely to make more money because the consumer has limited choice and must play your game. Moreover, the specialist has more control over the markets, which is advantageous given their rapid change. This preference for specialization doesn't mean, incidentally, that you can't do well as a commodity house; many can and do. But the secret in these instances lies primarily with efficient operations, which implies a large relative market share. Only a few can have this size advantage, though there are any number of smaller firms that are more efficient than their bigger cousins, and thus more profitable.

Both the CEO and the marketing manager of the emerging enterprise must pay very close attention to the results of their efforts to create the aura of specialization in their product line. One sometimes humbling experience is to practice telling friends and business associates, when they ask how your new business is getting along, the particular features of your product or service that, you believe, put it in the specialty category. If you find it difficult to put these precious facts into words that are easily understood, then you have a problem and it would be best to stop and do something about it right away.

If management's preference is for a specialty niche, and if the inexorable market drift is toward commodity, then the name of the game for management is to regain a specialty position:

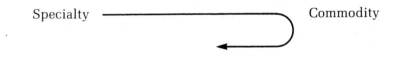

Specialty   Commodity

Let's call this the "bent arrow" definition of marketing. Marketing tries to regain a specialty position by turning the arrow back.

How is this done? How do firms escape the pull of the mature commodity world?

One way is through product innovation. Consider Apple's computer, Tektronix's oscilliscope, Procter and Gamble's fluoride-based toothpaste, Intel's microprocessor, and dozens more. These products represent technological breakthroughs that permit the innovator a limited time of market leadership. To be first in a new technology usually means to hold the specialist's cards. Who wouldn't want continuously such a product edge? Unfortunately, such ongoing leadership is virtually impossible. There is always that unknown inventor working in his garage who comes up with the better mousetrap. We haven't yet discovered a way to maintain a monopoly in technical brains. But as long as the product advantage lasts, technological innovation is a superb specialty approach.

We must be careful, however, not to be competely carried away with technical promptness. The innovator often pays dearly for his pioneering role. The primary demand investments are his, as are the investments needed to perfect the new technology. Some firms, accordingly, have preferred to wait and then come in wiser and richer for having watched the innovator. Texas Instruments and IBM are two examples of firms that are great copiers and executors.

Closely related to technology breakthroughs are product improvements and variations that satisfy significant customer values—the Nike shoe designs, the fuel-efficient Boeing 767, the throwaway pen, the self-sharpening saw chain, the higher-quality Northface mountaineering equipment. To the extent that product improvements are viewed by consumers as valuable, the producer's specialty hold is strengthened.

Some specialization is based on such intangibles as image, consumer perceptions, and brand recognition. You and I buy many items for these reasons—Gerber baby foods, Kodak cameras, Roman Meal bread, Schweppes tonic, Maxwell House coffee, Chevrolet automobiles, and any number of clothing items. How much is a little green alligator on your T-shirt worth? Or a "swoosh" on your jogging shoes? Or the Caterpillar service reputation?

Segmentation is another powerful marketing tool for creating market distinction. If you can better identify and satisfy the needs of particular customer groups, you can postpone the undifferentiated approach to mass markets. The more precisely a customer's needs are identified and met, the more secure the supplier's position. Procter and Gamble, for example, produces over ten brands of detergents and several toothpaste variations. Each is aimed at a singular portion of the market and, to the extent that the strategies are successful, results in specialty positions.

A general word of warning on segmentation: make certain through your early market studies that the segment of the market that you are planning to go after is in fact large enough to sustain not only your early production but a full-bore product introduction over the span of the next three to five years. Consider the truncated product lives of Polaroid movie cameras, Osborne portable computers, designer jeans, and hand-held video games.

Breakthroughs in distribution can also turn the arrow. L'eggs hosiery reversed a flat-to-declining hosiery trend with its novel distribution approach. So, too, did Timex and McDonald's as well as Sears Roebuck earlier with its catalog innovation. Consider additionally the use today of satellites for delivering TV signals as well as other forms of data, and the digitizing of voice and sound, which are radical improvements in distribution.

One of the more memorable specialty approaches has been that of Arm & Hammer with its baking soda. Can you think of anything you can't do with that product? It's a deodorant, an odor absorber for the refrigerator, a cooking ingredient, raw material for swimming pool filter systems, base material for cat litter, and so on. New uses are Arm & Hammer's marketing genius, which in turn opens up hitherto untapped specialty markets. Johnson's Baby Shampoo gained a large share of the adult market, and Honda changed the entire definition of the motorcycle. ("It's fun")—both new-use strategies to market traditional products.

Some firms have turned the arrow by raising prices, though often in combination with other changes (such as redesign). The fashion industry is illustrative, as is the market for diamonds. Steuben Glass, by means of creative design, high quality, and limited distribution, succeeded in gaining market share and premium prices for its glassware.

Packaging, for others, has been the path to uniqueness. The soft drink industry has competed aggressively for years on the basis of package variations, as have large sections of the canning and food industries. Who can deny the attractiveness of the flip-top box, the easy-open beer can, or the squeeze bottle for mustard? And how about the brillant market recovery of Tylenol with its security packaging?

We could no doubt double our list of effective marketing approaches to specialization—the reader's imagination is the only limitation. The point to remember is that there are many ingenious ways to ward off the commodity extreme. Effective marketing establishes a differential advantage in the marketplace.

Definition 2: The Activities of Marketing

Marketing consists of a number of business activities that collectively represent the firm's blueprint for acquiring customers. In large companies there would be a cadre of people for each activity; in smaller firms, particularly start-ups, there are fewer such specialists and sometimes there is only one, the very busy marketing executive.

These activities are what most practitioners call the *marketing mix* or "how the company intends to spend its marketing dollars."

The first two activities, we would contend, should always be market research and product planning—the first to identify and at times discover the markets and their needs, and the second to make sure the supplier meets these needs and defines his specialty. The remaining array of activities can be listed in any order that best reflects the chosen strategy. Such an array would normally include:

- Advertising
- Direct mail
- Merchandising
- Promotion
- Selling (and sales management)
- Distribution (or what the customer has to do to get the product)
- Service
- Pricing

These are the most obvious activities. There is no "complete" list because different companies, depending on their circumstances, have unique mixes. An instrument house, like Varian, will use application laboratories as important selling aids (if the lab can solve the prospect's problems with the company's instruments, a sale is likely to follow). Other firms, such as Motorola, will offer customer seminars (for education and persuasion) or rely heavily on trade shows, demonstrations, and traveling exhibits. Most high-technology firms can use successfully visits to headquarters to show off new products; consider Bell Labs in this regard.

Two observations should be made about the marketing mix definition. First, no one activity is synonymous with marketing. Sales is not marketing, nor is advertising, merchandising, or direct mail. Each is a subdivision of marketing, to be sure. But marketing is the entire collection and consists, therefore, of staff and line, planning and execution, short-term and long-term activities. It is surprising, nonetheless, how many companies continue to have a partial definition of marketing—such as selling, for example.

Second, the mix reflects the firm's most important operating assumption. When the marketing manager puts his budget together and allocates the funds among the mix alternatives, he is describing his interpretation of customer buying behavior. If the mix were not such an interpretation, it wouldn't make much sense. It would be, instead, a random collection of expenditures. As a result, it is critical, if you are the marketing manager, or if the manager reports to you, that you zero in on the customer buying assumptions. Why are you putting 20 percent of your funds into advertising? What is the role of the sales force in the strategy? What happens if a new segment enters the market? How will price changes affect the various segments? What is competition doing? Can you follow up the sales leads if you decide to exhibit?

Definition 3: Marketing as a Management Point of View

The third definition is more comprehensive, and has had major impact upon American business thinking. We label this definition the *marketing philosophy* and generally trace its roots to the General Electric Company as well as the early writings of Peter Drucker.

The marketing philosophy argues that there is only one way to run a company successfully: make sure that every activity (be it finance, production, transportation, selling, or R&D) has but a single purpose and is so judged, namely to satisfy customer requirements at a profit. It follows from this belief that the starting point for all business operations is the customer and his or her needs. Marketing creates customers by making sure that their needs are satisfied. This is an "outside-in" management orientation. The "inside-out" alternative is well illustrated in the classic marketing story about the drug company sales manager who called his sales force together and announced, "Here's the cure: now go find a disease!" Steve Allen, in his early days as an entertainer, had a similar ploy, "Here's the answer. Now what is the question?"

The marketing philosophy focuses on general management. It deals with the totality of operating a company. It makes intuitive sense because it is premised upon a truism: companies don't compete. There is no way a company can compete, whether it be Coke versus Pepsi, Boeing versus Douglas, or Macy's versus Gimbel's. *But people can and do compete!* The worker on the drill press, the laboratory technician, the financial analyst are as much in competition with their counterparts in other companies as are the salespeople in the field. Marketing, when viewed globally, consists of more than the marketing department: the entire firm's purpose is to create and satisfy the customers. Georges Clemenceau, the French statesman, once remarked, "War is too important to leave it to the generals." We are saying, "Marketing is too important to leave it to the marketing specialists."

This philosophy, as we stated above, has had considerable influence upon American business. The importance of the consumer is reasonably well understood and recognized, though some managements are more sensitive to the markets than others. Regardless, a great deal of lip service, at least, is paid to the urgency of being marketing-driven. As marketing practitioners, we are well aware that "out there" are potential customers with specific needs, perhaps overt, perhaps latent. All we have to do is identify these needs and satisfy them. We are dependent upon the existing demand!

But herein lies a practical problem. The marketing philosophy is a reactive viewpoint—find the needs and satisfy them. The market dictates. But is the world that one-way? Obviously not. It is filled with entrepreneurs who anticipate the market, who are proactive instead of reactive. These entrepreneurs apparently defy the logical need to analyze the markets and have succeeded with new imaginative approaches. Apparently there is a nonanalytic alternative. Can it be that serendipity is a viable concept? It most certainly is!

Step back for an instant and reconsider our standard systematic approach to marketing. It starts with the implicit assumption that the manager must rely upon market research, product planning, segmentation, and rigorous product strategies to capitalize on the existing opportunity. The focus is upon a deductive, analytic marketing program. Over time, such firms should show a nice growth rate:

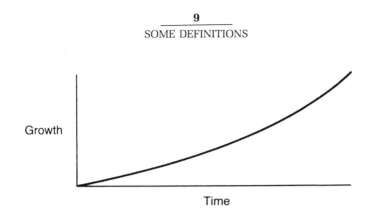

But although analysis is an important element in the equation, it is only part of it. Analysis has a serious deficiency. How about those exceptional companies that appear to break through without much careful analysis and planning? To illustrate, here is a simplified growth curve for a high-technology firm:

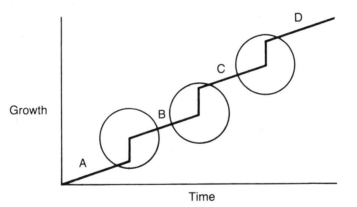

Notice the circled quantum breakthroughs where the firm jumps from level of activity A to level of activity B or C or D. A close look at these jumps reveals that they are typically the result of the introduction of innovative new products—Varian's NMR spectrometer, Versatec's electrostatic printer, the Apple II, the microprocessor—products invented by creative geniuses who depended upon more than analytic information about markets. Theirs was a burst of inspiration that revolutionized the existing state of the art. As we have seen, moreover, significant breakthroughs are not restricted to technology: they can occur in distribution, packaging, service, or market segmentation.

Creativity is an essential element of growth. Unfortunately, it is sloppy and unpredictable; it is nonanalytic. Creativity is hard to forecast, to control, to originate. For managers the decision problem is "How much of my resources do I put into the analytic approach, how much into the intuitive?" Neither extreme alone would make much sense. Analytic by itself means that you will probably miss the great growth opportunities; creative alone means that the odds favor your going bankrupt.

Maybe the ratio should be 80/20 (analytic/creative), maybe 70/30. Whatever the current proportions, the split is crucial. The marketing manager should modify the marketing philosophy to include the creative element and then, by being close to his customers, spawn new ideas and innovative approaches.

For the emerging company, sound attitudes and philosophies about customers and markets need to be carefully nurtured. Unlike the well-established company with its existing culture, the emerging firm does not have a culture of time and common experience. This thrusts onto the already busy CEO another important duty: setting the tone, and establishing the goals—creating the kind of corporate culture the company will want to work in from now on. This is the time to make clear how customers should be dealt with, how they should be treated on returns, or credits, or damaged goods, or late deliveries or payments.

Keep in mind that these are *marketing* details and issues. How they are treated, or dismissed, creates a code of conduct or culture within the organization. Think these through from a profit-conscious, marketing mind-set, not through the eyes of the controller or office manager. The importance of this approach is demonstrated in the real-life experiences recounted below.

General Foods in the late 1950s was a superb marketing machine under Charles Mortimer and "Tex" Cook. Every known marketing device and method was used for such emerging products as frozen foods, decaffeinated coffee, and the first synthetic foods, like Tang orange drink. Market research was painstaking and thorough. The General Foods kitchens under Ellen Ann Dunham were very consumer-oriented. Product managers worked hard and were promptly and publicly rewarded or punished. The four best advertising agencies made important contributions.

Even so, occasionally a competitor came up with a better package or campaign or, heaven forbid, product. In these circumstances Mortimer was merciless. "Develop our answer now. The best plans can and do go wrong. I expect you to 'scrounge' for answers which will hold the fort until we can make the necessary changes in our master plans and product programs. It is up to the marketing management not to lose share whatever happens." This was a clear statement of his expectations, in a real-world environment. Moreover, he continually exhorted his marketing people to go out and find out what the store manager and customers wanted, including the Gaines dog food consumers.

Robert Wilson, well-known turn-around CEO, has a very simple dictum: "Love your product." If marketing management is really enthusiastic and enamored of its product, this attitude will shine through. Under this atmosphere of undying affection, there is no room for the blasé market researcher or careless plant manager. The tone is set. Each person is expected to be proud of, and anxious for, that precious product. As Wilson said, "When you win it should be the thrill of your life, but when you lose you should cry a lot and then fix whatever caused the loss." He expected marketeers and engineers to work Saturdays and Sundays if things were not going according to plan. Clearly this is good advice for the marketing team of the emerging company. Moreover, it is important leadership philosophy.

Whether troubleshooting for General Foods or "loving" the products of a company struggling to turn around, these executives shared an important insight. Corporate executives should communicate to their staff concern for product quality and customer concerns. In each case these superior managers solved their corporate problems by viewing them through a marketing-oriented focus.

Definition 4: Marketing as Viewed by the Senior Executive

Finally, we can look at marketing through the eyes of the general manager and ask, "What should senior management expect from marketing? How should the function be judged by those who direct the enterprise?"

There are three contributions that marketing should make to the enterprise: *direction, strategy,* and *making the sale* (in the persuasion sense of the word)—all presumably with optimal gross profits.

Direction has to do with "Where are we going?," "Where will we be in five years?," "What are the opportunity areas that should be tapped—the technologies, the markets, the applications?," "Where does competition seem to be headed?"

We hasten to add, at this point, that we are using *marketing* in the philosophical sense of the word, not the functional. Thus, in a high-technology firm direction is likely to come from R&D, whereas a packaged consumer goods house will probably rely upon careful market research and the marketing department. (In point of fact, direction might come from any number of other functional areas, depending on the circumstances.) Whatever the genesis, that source should have an ongoing interface with the markets. Some R&D departments pass this interface test well, but many more do not. If R&D fails to perceive the market, then the company runs the risk of being led into blind alleys: into markets that are technically interesting, state-of-the-art, but economic disasters. Or the R&D department may champion products that can't be handled profitably by production and other functions of the business or are too far ahead of the customers' expectations or willingness to experiment. In this regard consider the "far-out" Chrysler of the 1930s or the picture phone of AT&T.

The marketing department, of course, can be guilty of similar errors, particularly those of championing uneconomic projects. Additionally, marketing practitioners all too often have short time horizons and favor the immediate. Quotas are broken up into limited periods—one quarter, six months, maybe one year. In department stores, for example, comparisons are typically made with "same day or week, last year."

Remaining aware of these potential weaknesses, the general manager should expect from marketing specific assistance in deciding future direction, both near and long term.

Strategy, the second contribution of marketing, concentrates upon the question "How are we going to get there?" The strategy is the blueprint for realizing the sales objectives—the basis on which we intend to compete. In almost all instances, except commodities, we do have strategic options. Strategy is, in the literal sense, a resource allocation decision. How much money for advertising, selling, sales promotion? The marketing mix, of course, is a description of the strategy.

But this definition leaves something to be desired; it misses the essence of effective strategy. Strategy is "How do I get more than my fair share?"—whatever that might mean. Anyone can get his or her fair share, but it takes a differential advantage to gain the upper hand. This is the *edge*. The edge can involve uniqueness in any of the mix variables, or in more effective execution. Many a successful strategy is the result primarily of superior performance. The general manager should expect from marketing a working strategy being implemented by an enthusiastic team.

Finally, marketing makes a profitable sale. Even with the best direction and distinctive strategy, the sale will not be realized without effective persuasion—be it by salespeople, advertising, sales promotion, or distributors. Making the sale is, needless to say, the operating dimension of marketing. It is often referred to as the tactics. Regardless of label, nothing really happens until a sale is made.

It is a truism that some people can sell and others couldn't even buy their way out of a paper bag. Selling is a distinct and separate skill that requires training and retraining, stimulation and motivation. As Mr. Watson (senior) used to say, a salesman is a man who sells. Thus the general manager should look to his marketing function to make sales competitively in even the toughest situations.

Direction, strategy, and persuasion have been described above as if they were discrete elements, somehow interrelated but separate. That's not quite true; it is not easy to distinguish one from the other at the margin. Where does direction stop and strategy begin? Strategy, as we shall see, is in fact a function of direction. If we elect to grow in a particular business or market, strategies are shaped by that decision. Strategies, in addition, dictate the nature of the tactics, and the dividing line between strategy and tactics is always thin.

Notwithstanding, the notion of a tripartite whole is a useful intellectual invention and helps to highlight the major dimensions of the field. And it is around these three dimensions that the quality of a company's marketing function can be measured.

WHAT IS YOUR MARKETING SCORE?

This is probably a good time to let you measure the performance of your marketing unit. How do you stack up? However, instead of relying upon our three gross measures of direction, strategy, and persuasion, we have detailed a number of quite specific questions pulled from all three. The questions are those that are pertinent when viewing a business enterprise through marketing glasses. The list, as you shall see, ranges rather broadly but, we would maintain, represents a reasonable sampling of marketing matters.

We should make it clear that this is not a really serious test. It is meant to be provocative. Consider its shortcomings:

1. All the questions are of equal value.

2. The scoring system is arbitrary and subjective.

3. The interpretation of acceptable and unacceptable grades is a matter of convenience.

4. There are several "value systems" built into a few of the questions—and our value systems may differ from yours.

5. We have assumed that you produce a product. If service is your output, then you'll have to change a few words in some of the questions.

But have a run at it. Rank your marketing operation on a simple scale: 0 if it is poor; 1 if it is adequate; 2 if it is strong. The "perfect score" is 100: fifty questions (number 5 has four parts) at 2 points maximum each.

What Is Your Marketing Score?

1. Does the company have a clearly understood goal (i.e., business definition)? 2 – 1 – 0

2. Does the business definition influence the behavior of the people in the organization? 2 – 1 – 0

3. Are your employees aware of the company's essential (basic) knack? i.e., What is the company really good at? 2 – 1 – 0

4. Does the company make full use of its strengths? 2 – 1 – 0

5. Can you and your subordinate managers answer the following questions?

   a. What is the effect upon profits of changes in product mix, volume, and selling prices? 2 – 1 – 0

   b. Where are the key points at which the company adds significant consumer values? 2 – 1 – 0

   c. What is the return on the assets you employ? 2 – 1 – 0

   d. What are the direct and variable costs, and the break-even point? 2 – 1 – 0

6. Does the company have a growth plan based upon trends and opportunities? 2 – 1 – 0

7. Does planning input come up from the ranks? 2 – 1 – 0

8. Are 50% of your sales the result of new additions (products, new markets) in the past five years? 2 – 1 – 0

9. Are your objectives specific and measurable, financial and competitive?   2 – 1 – 0

10. Does management know its share of market and the value of one share point?   2 – 1 – 0

11. Is the market strategy clear in terms of product definition, segment identification, price policy, communication strategy, and delivery system strategy?   2 – 1 – 0

12. Are new product and new account development specifically accounted for (i.e., is someone responsible)?   2 – 1 – 0

13. Does the firm take full advantage of the small number of customers, managers, and personnel who account for the bulk of the results?   2 – 1 – 0

14. Does the company reward creativity and innovation?   2 – 1 – 0

15. Are the strategies of the chief competitors well known and understood?   2 – 1 – 0

16. Does higher management operate by exception, or does it get involved in minutiae?   2 – 1 – 0

17. Is there a market research function that actively studies markets and opportunities?   2 – 1 – 0

18. Are the outstanding performers compensated in proportion to their competence?   2 – 1 – 0

19. Are key managers compensated for both long- and short-term performance?   2 – 1 – 0

20. Does the company have an ongoing feedback system from the marketplace?   2 – 1 – 0

21. Are prices a function of customer values (rather than costs)?   2 – 1 – 0

22. Does the company know its segments (customer classes) and their buying criteria?   2 – 1 – 0

23. Is compensation based upon making the plan (rather than *how* the plan is made)?   2 – 1 – 0

24. Does the company compete on the basis of total buyer values (or is the physical product the only variable of importance)?   2 – 1 – 0

25. Does the marketing strategy specifically state whether:

    a. The objective is to gain awareness, trial, or repeat?   2 – 1 – 0

b. The objective is to penetrate the present market, obtain more usage, new uses, or new customers?   2 – 1 – 0

26. Are there contingency plans?   2 – 1 – 0

27. Does management drop obsolete products and markets rapidly (or does management retain them unduly)?   2 – 1 – 0

28. Are the managers having fun?   2 – 1 – 0

29. Does promotion depend upon performance (or upon age)?   2 – 1 – 0

30. Does the management have a plan over time for retaining its specialty position?   2 – 1 – 0

31. Is management aware of the elasticity (i.e., impact upon sales) of the various items in the mix, including price, promotion, distribution, availability, credibility, credit, etc.?   2 – 1 – 0

32. Is the form of organization designed to better service customers (or is it designed for internal convenience)?   2 – 1 – 0

33. Do lower management echelons get a constant chance to state their opinions?   2 – 1 – 0

34. Are assignments specific enough so that blame and credit can be determined?   2 – 1 – 0

35. Are the managers action-oriented (or philosophy-oriented)?   2 – 1 – 0

36. Do managers fight to change the status quo (or accept it)?   2 – 1 – 0

37. Are there specific plans to enhance the product values over time in order to forestall the product life cycle?   2 – 1 – 0

38. Are the firm's "marketing messages" understood (i.e., those variables that attract or repel customers)?   2 – 1 – 0

39. Does the firm grow to an overall logic (or for growth's sake)?   2 – 1 – 0

40. Is there a systematic plan to develop managers?   2 – 1 – 0

41. Are incompetent managers removed (or tolerated)?   2 – 1 – 0

42. Does the firm attempt to build markets (or to tap existing markets)?   2 – 1 – 0

43. Is management proactive (or reactive)?   2 – 1 – 0

44. Does the accounting system provide management data (as opposed to financial data)? I.e., Are marginal costs clear? Contribution percentages? Fixed and variable costs?   2 – 1 – 0

45. Is the overall management thrust one of innovation (or "me-tooism")?   2 – 1 – 0

46. Is there esprit, excitement, within the organization?   2 – 1 – 0

$$Maximum = 50 \times 2 = 100 \; points$$

Star	= 85–100
Strong performer	= 70–85
Weak performer	= 50–70
Not so hot	= Under 50

SUMMARY

Marketing can be viewed, usefully, from four vantage points:

1. The methods by which a firm tries to regain a specialty position.
2. A series of management activities, described as "the mix."
3. A management philosophy that emphasizes a customer-oriented approach, modified by creativity.
4. The general manager's vehicle for obtaining direction, strategy, and completed sales.

2

Consumer Goods, Industrial Goods, and Services: Differences and Similarities

Marketing, like any other business function, has two dimensions, conceptual and application-specific. Therefore, we must in practice deal with such all-purpose ideas as product life cycles, segmentation, and the customer adoption cycle as well as such situational specifics as how to pay computer salespeople, forecast the sales of our toothpaste, or establish discounts for our particular channels of distribution.

The reader can easily recognize the problems in writing this book: do we concentrate on the conceptual at the risk of being unduly theoretical, or do we concentrate on the specific trees at the risk of missing the forest? There is no obvious answer, and it is too simple to say that we shall do both. The balance between the two remains an important decision. Our bias is to favor a strong conceptual base on the theory that the emerging company needs a Christmas tree first on which to hang its ornaments. It has been our teaching experience that most managers can translate the concepts into the idiom of their particular world. At the same time, and in order to be as practical as possible, we shall use a number of "for instances."

There is, at the outset, one fundamental issue that, on the surface, seems to restrict our decision to stress the conceptual. Don't we have to provide different structures for consumer goods, industrial goods, and service companies? Surely they are not the same, and it would seem mandatory that we regularly offer different examples for the three classifications. The need for such separate treatment is certainly a recognized part of marketing folklore. We usually think of the marketing jobs in Lever Brothers, General Electric, and American Express as essentially different. It isn't common, in the real world, for managers to switch back and forth over their careers from market type to market type.

That is too bad, because it means that we may be denying our firms a promising pool of potential marketing recruits. Packaged consumer goods companies, to be specific, are oriented toward marketing and have traditionally developed strong product managers. High-tech companies, on the other hand, turn out research and technical people with perhaps some selling skill. Might not a technical company have better luck recruiting marketing expertise from outside its industry, where the applicant pool is larger? Unfortunately, it is common practice in these technical industries to place primary emphasis upon technical know-how rather than customer applications. This doesn't mean, of course, that some haven't tried. There have indeed been some successful cross-fertilization attempts. A few of the large banks, to cite an example, have attempted to introduce product management talent from the consumer goods companies. Nike, a successful athletic shoe producer, insists on hiring generalists and has had great luck with lawyers and accountants in top management. Many a semiconductor start-up in Silicon Valley has recognized also the early need for generalist ability as opposed to a rigid insistence upon highly specialized engineers. Apple Computer, with its appointment of John Scully from Pepsico as president, is an interesting example.

THE PROBLEM OF STEREOTYPES

One result of market compartmentalization is that we have developed stereotypes of each, some flattering, some not, depending upon our particular leaning. For example, industrial marketing is rational, technical, complex, sales-oriented, service-dependent, reliable, respectable, and honest. Consumer marketing is emotional, flaky, based on image and advertising, concerned with perceptions, distribution-oriented, biased toward merchandising and ambience, and dominated by product management. Service marketing, in its turn, is fuzzy, personal, ethereal, in need of rationalization, low in productivity, hard to get your hands on, devoid of good distribution channels, one-on-one, and people-dependent.

That these generalizations are only partly true, and in some instances totally untrue, is not always recognized. And yet:

- Consumer goods are not a homogeneous set. There are vast differences, for example, among consumer durables (white goods, automobiles, furniture), consumer capital goods (houses), services (insurance, health care, education), and such disposables as food and drugs. Surely the consumer market stereotype fits badly this diverse array of products.

- Industrial goods have the same characteristic of heterogeneity. Do we consider as similar supplies, components, motors, transistors, equipment, and plant?

- Services are even more diverse—software, time-share, medical exams, accounting audits, transportation, education, entertainment, restaurants, recreation, and dieting.

Professor Dan Thomas has classified usefully the wide variety of so-called services and highlights this diversity (see Figure 2.1).[1]

To treat the three markets as mutually exclusive further ignores those companies that cut across the lines. How about the mainframe producer that provides software and technical service? Or the food manufacturer (Pillsbury) that operates a number of restaurants, or a General Electric with divisions that make generators, refrigerators, nuclear reactors, and hundreds of other items and services?

FIGURE 2.1

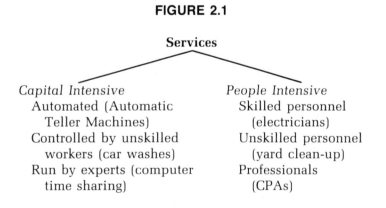

Capital Intensive	People Intensive
Automated (Automatic Teller Machines)	Skilled personnel (electricians)
Controlled by unskilled workers (car washes)	Unskilled personnel (yard clean-up)
Run by experts (computer time sharing)	Professionals (CPAs)

---

[1] Derived from Dan R. E. Thomas, "Strategy Is Different in Service Businesses," *Harvard Business Review*, July–August 1978, pp. 158–65.

A final complication in reducing consumer, industrial, and service firms to stereotypes is that many successful companies succeed with "unnatural strategies." How about the consumer goods company that sells direct to its customers—for example, Tupperware, Mary Kay, or Avon? Or the industrial company that sells through its own retail stores (IBM) or telemarketing (Goodrich)? Some of the more effective marketing strategies are those that make use of nontraditional channels, advertising approaches, or pricing strategies.

THE COMMON FICTION

Having recognized these complications, it is, notwithstanding, worth reviewing the real and imagined differences among the three markets. There are some important differences and equally some important similarities. The table on page 22 is designed to summarize the major points of contrast that many argue exist, though the careful reader will recognize that the differences become more tentative and less convincing as the eye progresses down the page. Putting it another way, one can probably find as many exceptions to the rule deep into the exhibit as there is substantiating evidence.

Notice also that the three columns are closely defined, that is, restricted to three specific kinds of products and services. This means that the real-life rich mixture of variations within each column are overlooked.

Some of the differences are significant, some are of minor marketing importance. We believe that the most meaningful have to do with the mass markets of the consumer goods companies, the technology of the industrial suppliers, and the intangibility of the service operations.

If the reader accepts the notion of three contrasting market situations, it is useful to pose the question, "What are the critical management talents required for each market?" The mass markets of the consumer goods companies, with the attendant reliance upon advertising and mass distribution systems, suggest the need for communication and merchandising talents. The Hewlett-Packards of this world, on the other hand, need considerable sales management and service skills as well as management's ability to translate technical concepts into applications. The service-based manager is more difficult to characterize. He or she must certainly be adept at ensuring personal satisfaction among the customers. Additionally, the service-based manager has the need to communicate to the potential user in concrete terms what his

Some Marketing Differences, Real and Presumed

PACKAGED CONSUMER GOODS	INDUSTRIAL INSTRUMENTS	COMMERCIAL AIR SERVICE
1. Heavy pull (advertising) supplemented with point of sale and push efforts	Heavy push (salespeople) supported by service and some advertising	Pull (advertising plus word of mouth) plus reliance upon personal experience
2. Emphasis on mass markets	Highly segmented markets—limited customers	Concentration on business traveler—use other audiences for incremental income
3. Impersonal emphasis: advertising, brand names, perceptions, self-service	Personal emphasis: service/backup support, confidence, salespeople	Impersonal pull plus in-flight personal attention
4. Purchaser's risk is in product satisfaction	Purchaser's risk is in product performance, service, and technical support	Purchaser's risk is in on-time delivery of service and personal satisfaction
5. Segmentation by groups	Segmentation by individual account with some group classification	Segmented by business and nonbusiness grouping
6. Innovation includes more than product: package, promotions/deals, perceptions, communication	Innovation more product-related: technology, financing, availability, support systems	Innovation lies in price deals and promotions, excellence of personal service, schedules
7. Communication efforts are highly leveraged (many customers see one ad)	Low leverage—essentially one-on-one relationship	Low leverage, complicated by fact that product can't be inventoried
8. Price focuses on volume—repeat purchases	Price focuses on per-transaction profit	Price for repeat purchase and incremental income
9. Few influencers in buying decision	Many influencers; multiple roles	Few influencers: less predictable
10. Short decision process	Long decision process	Short process
11. Heavy brand switching	Less likely to switch: institutional constraints	Loyal, but once turned off, difficult to recapture
12. Short memories	Long memories	Long memories
13. Customer may not be consumer	End user likely to be the customer	Customer is often the end user, but travel agent is a critical intermediary
14. Tangible product	Tangible product	Much intangibility

or her sometimes rather nebulous service is all about. Confidence creation and response time are fundamental in the service environment.

These management requirements lie at the heart of the debate: "Are different marketing individuals needed for each market?" Not entirely. Most of the major marketing ideas, such as diffusion theory or product positioning, cut across the lines and have general applicability. At the same time, however, the specific marketing mix variables are situational. As a consequence, whether or not the individual manager .can be rotated back and forth is dependent on how much specific knowledge is needed and how long it will take to acquire it. At one extreme, the manager may need the technical expertise of an electrical engineer or a nuclear physicist. For a management position it will take considerable time to acquire a working knowledge of these disciplines, though much shorter than earning a college degree. More often the requisite knowledge requirements deal with customer applications and market requirements, needs that all marketing managers must deal with. Our conclusion is that marketing managers have more mobility than imagined, but they must learn the vocabulary. The higher in management one goes, the more transferable the personnel. It's easier, in other words, to cross-fertilize a marketing vice-president than a sales supervisor.

THE SPECIAL CASE OF SERVICES

Having said all this, a case can still be made that the differences between consumer goods and industrial goods are much less than the differences between goods and services—that is, between tangibles and intangibles. Instead of spending our time contrasting the consumer manager with the industrial, the argument goes, we should more properly be concerned with the idiosyncrasies of marketing services. Not only are services unique but they dominate American business. Services make up more than half of our industrial income and therefore warrant special attention.

The nature of physical products simplifies the task of managing. In elementary terms, physical products have two distinguishing attributes: (1) they are produced in one location and consumed in another (e.g., the factory is in Palo Alto but the market is international) and (2) they are produced today but consumed tomorrow.

These attributes mean that production and consumption can have separate cycles (the inventory is the cushion); a quality-control gate at the plant ensures that the bad product doesn't get into the market;

the consumer can be kept out of the factory and therefore can't affect the manufacturing process; and there can be two separate groups of employees, production and marketing. The fact that the two functions can be separated is a great convenience and provides management with considerable flexibility.

But consider such services as air transportation. The convenient division between marketing and operations (e.g., "manufacturing") is not as evident. Production and consumption occur at the same time and in the same place. What, for example, does the airline produce? It is movement from city A to city B, at a particular time. When we, as fliers, consume the service, we fly on that same plane and at that same time. Production and consumption are simultaneous.

Hence we can't inventory the output. The empty flight is empty forever. We can't put on a quality-control gate prior to consumption— the cabin attendants (operations) have direct contact with the customers. And we certainly can't keep the passengers "out of the factory." The clients are all seated there and are, in a real sense, part of the "product." The rowdy drunk or the squalling infant can spoil the trip for all. Quality control is not fully in the producer's hands. Finally, the simultaneous nature of production and consumption makes it awkward at best to separate the two functions. They overlap so much that the best course of action is to train each functional specialist to be like the other. The cabin attendant is part of the service package that the consumer buys.

It may help to summarize some of the more common distinctions:

1. Goods can be inventoried; services can't.
2. The customers' perceptions of goods are more concrete and specific than their perceptions of services, which are fuzzy.
3. Service marketing is more often than not a personal process.
4. The customer is often part of the service, which complicates the quality-control issue (consider the patient getting a yearly medical checkup).
5. Employees can be neatly pigeonholed as "production" or "marketing" in the physical-goods world.

The label "service," however, as we stated earlier, is too sweeping a generalization. Its heterogeneity leads to the warning that simplifying descriptions, as in the case of the airline, must be approached with care. To be sure, there are many services that fit this definition: medical examinations, education, the theater and entertainment, and restaurants come to mind. On the other hand, some services aren't particularly personal (such as electric utilities and time-share systems), and some can separate the customer from the process (power generation)—but almost all suffer from the inability to inventory their output.

This means that the idiosyncratic marketing task in services is to balance supply and demand *in the short run*. The short-run constraint is important for our purposes because long-term supply-and-demand balance is the concern of both product and service companies. How many plants? How many airplanes? How many cars for rent? These are balance questions that both sets of managements must address.

In the emerging company the dilemma is even more acute since there has not been a sufficient amount of experience to determine rationally the balance between capacity and expected sales. Here again the close watch of senior management upon the customers and their habits is absolutely essential. We are all aware of the fact that a good restaurant maintains its reputation and its excellence because the owner is there watching every meal being prepared and served. It is only when he delegates this personal supervision and watchful eye to someone less committed to the success of the venture that trouble starts. Here is certainly a basic point to be remembered by the emerging company.

The distinctive service dilemma, therefore, is the short-term one: given a certain capacity, how can equilibrium between output and sales be maintained when there is no inventory cushion?

There are a number of effective marketing approaches to this question of balance, some of which attack the supply side of the equation, and some the demand.

Supply can be stretched, for example, if consumers can be induced to participate in the process (e.g., clean their own tables at the fast-food establishment, assemble income tax data for the tax professional) or lower their expectations of acceptable service (so that the supply will stretch further). Some services, such as law and medicine, reassign routine tasks to paralegal and paramedical associates, thus freeing up the specialists for the critical tasks. Part-timers can also be used, as in the case of Christmas help at Macy's. McDonald's has excelled at mechanizing its approach to preparing and serving food so that the most unskilled labor can be employed. Some auto service operators use diagnostic equipment that eliminates most of the human skill.

Balancing the customer load is another solution, as in the case of requiring appointments, accepting reservations, or having travel agents bunch the flow of paperwork.

Demand manipulation can also help to maintain balance. Utilities will offer special prices for "off-peak" patronage, and the post office advertises that we should "mail early." Hotels build weekend trade by special promotional packages, and transportation companies go to great lengths today to attract marginal travelers, who can fill an otherwise empty seat. A bar attached to a restaurant helps to spread the dining room rush.

Marketing strategy for the service operator, as we have shown, places a heavy premium upon short-run expediency (as well as long-term strategy).

SERVICES AND GOODS AS A CONTINUUM

A useful distinction was made in a 1978 article by G. Lynn Shostack, at the time a vice-president of Citibank.[2] She was concerned that services and goods were dichotomized as opposites (airplanes versus instruments), which led to the common conclusion that generalizations were impractical or had to be modified with a string of exceptions, as illustrated earlier in this chapter. Shostack's suggestion was to recognize that all goods and services fall along the following continuum:

Tangible $\longrightarrow$ Intangible

It is her contention that the output of companies can be positioned at different locations on this scale. An expensive automobile, for example, is more than rubber, metal, and upholstery: it carries an image of prestige, comfort, service, and dependability. Likewise, an intangible such as a college education is not entirely intangible—there are buildings, classroom seats, and books, all highly tangible. In fact, Shostack earmarked a number of products and services, whose positioning she hypothesized including salt at the tangible extreme and teaching at the other.

The accuracy of such placements is, no doubt, somewhat subjective. But Shostack then introduces a much more provocative idea: when

---

[2] Lynn G. Shostack, "Breaking Free from Product Marketing," *Journal of Marketing,* April 1977, pp. 73–80.

communicating about your product or service to the markets, use the approach of "opposites." Describe an intangible tangibly and a tangible intangibly. Thus, TWA doesn't sell "floating through space" but rather 747 airplanes, tasty meals, and attractive cabin attendants. And Revlon, with its tangible product line, sells hope, not cosmetics.

Shostack's argument is intuitively appealing. An intangible suffers from an unclear, nebulous perception. Intangibles, when described, don't mean the same thing to all listeners. Therefore the advertiser must give specific examples of what the service is all about—modern airplanes, desirable meals, helpful attendants. Conversely, a tangible item needs some broader appeal—some pizzazz. Differentiation should be in terms of nonphysical images and values.

These concepts are all very interesting and thought-provoking. But how does one bring them down to earth into the actuality of the marketplace?

Those successful companies which have a customer and marketing orientation do this, particularly in the service industries, by constantly training and reorienting their employees who are faced with a consuming public. Consumers can be contrary, as any retail clerk, waiter, or rent-a-car counter attendant can tell you. It is not human nature to smile in the face of adversity. It is really not a normal reaction to excuse yourself when the customer is at fault. The company that makes these episodes fun, that addresses them as specific examples and problems in the day-to-day servicing of its customer base, will succeed. The use of house organs, letters, and bulletin boards to publicly recognize special treatment by your employees is a must if you are going to preserve this necessary attitude. It is not sufficient to train an employee once on the niceties of customer handling. Training is continuous, particularly as customers become more sophisticated and accustomed to your product. Nordstrom's, a highly successful and fast-moving department store chain, has built much of its success on hiring salespeople who "like other people." Customer service at Nordstrom's is what we all reminisce about.

SUMMARY

It is possible, within useful boundaries, to generalize about marketing in consumer, industrial, and service companies. There are some differences, to be sure, among the three, but there is even more similarity especially in the applicability of key marketing concepts.

Definitions are a stumbling block that complicate the task of comparing the three markets. What is a consumer good? An industrial? A service?

Services are undeniably the most bothersome to prototype because they vary so enormously. In many cases, however, the inability to inventory services is the most important difference that distinguishes services from products. Marketing must cope with the ongoing task of keeping short-term supply and demand in balance.

Particularly in the services, it is mandatory that marketing create favorable employee attitudes about the customers. Companies that can ignite this spark of customer satisfaction, and keep it vibrant over the years, are those that will reap the lion's share. Common courtesy is still the bedrock of customer preferences.

It helps considerably to think less about three distinct market types and more about the concept of tangible goods and intangibles. All goods and services are a composite of tangibles and intangibles, not an assortment of "either/ors." The best advice for the emerging company is to recognize the "true" composition of output and communicate in terms of "opposites."

3

The Business Definition and Its Importance

There's a classic old joke about the pilot who announced, "I've got bad news and good news. We're lost, but we're making good time!"

The implication for the emerging company is all too apparent— new firms often grow at a rapid rate, but without direction. They don't know where they're going. It doesn't take much imagination to guess how such trips will probably end.

It is important, therefore, that the emerging company make a clear statement about its business, its direction, and its goals. Without such guidelines there is no way the rest of management can make sensible decisions about their strategies and tactics. There's many a middle manager who complains, "I wish they'd tell me what we're trying to do!"

It all starts with a definition: "What business are we in?" That definition is the underpinning for strategy, operating policies, employee morale ("Why should I work for this outfit?"), evaluation systems, stockholder excitement, and growth alternatives. The definition is the single most important task of the chief executive. And a thoughtful definition is doubly critical for the emerging enterprise, which needs to assemble its entire infrastructure.

Selecting the business definition is not easy, as anyone who has tried can verify. Nonetheless, it is an essential prerequisite and of vital interest to all functions of the company. Because our focus in this book is upon marketing, we shall concentrate our observations upon the linkage between marketing and business definition.

The first point to emphasize is that the business definition is the single most important determinant of marketing strategy. Strategy is dependent upon this definition, and it is dependent whether the definition is explicit or implicit. Furthermore, if there is no clear definition, that is unfortunately a statement in itself. So management might as well be explicit and know what it's doing!

WHAT BUSINESS AM I IN?

Professor Theodore Levitt wrote his classic piece, "Marketing Myopia," in 1958.[1] He took the position that too many firms fail because they have a myopic definition of their business. The movie companies viewed themselves as being in the film business instead of entertainment and hence left the field to television. The railroads, similarly, were in railroading rather than transportation, and the petroleum companies in petroleum instead of energy—all of which, it should be noted, is easier said after the fact. You may not agree with all of Levitt's points, but the fact remains that he helped establish the conceptual and practical importance of carefully defining the business. The way employees behave, for example, is a reflection of this definition. But the definition can be elusive. For example, is a retailer the seller for the manufacturer or the buyer for the consumer? The impact upon the behavior of the employees will clearly be influenced by the decision. Is Getty Synthetic Fuel in the business of collecting, processing, and selling methane ("natural") gas from landfills, or is it in the methane emission and pollution control business? Wouldn't the answer similarly alter behavior?

There is a case we use often in teaching that illustrates well this requirement for defining the business and how that definition shapes marketing strategy.[2] Harlan was a producer of basic chemicals for the paper industry. For many good reasons management decided to diversify and considered several alternatives. One, the mining of dominite, appeared particularly attractive. Although there were other known deposits of dominite, this would be the first domestic exploitation. Dominite is a talc-like raw material that, research tests indicated, outperformed talc (when used in the right proportions) in the making of such products as ceramic wall tile. In fact, the blend of talc and dominite called for

---

[1] Theodore Levitt, "Marketing Myopia," reprint from the *Harvard Business Review*, September–October 1975, no. 75507.

[2] Harlan Chemical Corporation, ICH 9-574-011, Harvard Business School Case Services, Harvard Business School, Boston, MA 02163.

less time in the kilns, and resulted in better finishes, better coloring, and less cracking, all favorable factors in terms of profits. On the other hand, the tile manufacturer would have to replace dies at an average cost of $500,000. There was no free lunch. All in all, however, the economics of the switch appeared reasonable for the tile manufacturer.

Some pencil pushing further indicated to Harlan management that their chances for making a profit were good. Under some reasonable cost and price assumptions, a nice 15 percent ROI could be realized if dominite sales reached only 5 percent of the total talc market. So Harlan acquired the mine and spent, over the next three years, several million dollars launching the new product. Sales, unfortunately, never surpassed one half of one percent of talc sales, which meant the enterprise took a significant loss and the new management team was in great trouble. What went wrong?

Most class discussions wander around, and the students have considerable difficulty zeroing in on the fundamental reasons for failure. As a last resort it helps for the instructor to announce, "Let's go back to day one, when the company purchased the mine, and ask ourselves, 'What business are we in and what difference does it make?' " Typically the students will come up with a number of alternative business definitions, usually including:

(1) Mining	(2) Working with the tile manufacturer to increase his profits	(3) Developing better end products for the consumer

Notice the range of these three: from "mining" on the left, through the intermediary or customer in the center, to the ultimate consumer on the right (these three, of course, are only a sample of what might be proposed, but they do cover a meaningful spectrum). The students are then asked to consider each of the three definitions separately: "If these are the business definition choices, would the implied marketing strategy vary among them?" It would, to be sure! The mining (or hardware) point of view suggests a marketing strategy that includes long-term contracts, large-volume purchases, constant availability, sales to specifications, specified delivery conditions, and pricing by grade. Research, to consider another aspect of the operations, would undoubtedly deal with extraction and processing.

But consider, as other definitional alternatives, the customer and/or the consumer focus. In the second column the seller would send out a technical salesman to call on a technical buyer. All of the attributes of industrial selling would prevail: technical interface, application support, field service, close liaison between the engineering departments, special designs, and so on. When the consumer is the primary consideration, as in our final column, the seller is involved in all aspects of consumer marketing—market research, product planning, advertising and merchandising, distributor channels, service, and. so forth.

The three business definitions, as we can readily see, have called for three different strategies. Interestingly, the production process remains unchanged across the three: the dominite must be mined, processed, bagged, and transported regardless. In other words, the business definition is a management option. Hence our earlier reminder that the primary determinant of marketing strategy is the way the business is defined.

The Harlan example is easy to parallel. Consider, as a further illustration, a bottler of soft drinks trying to decide on emphasis. Could the bottler not use a similar format to Harlan's?

(1) Moving fluid   (2) Developing a strong distribution system ("If the retailer does well, I'll do well.")   (3) Building end markets ("So I'll hire a youth coordinator and sponsor picnics.")

Again we can deduce the appropriate strategies. In #1 the bottler would prefer a pipeline from his line to your house! In #2 his concentration will be upon dealer needs: display, packaging, cooperative advertising, merchandising, and promotions—a "push" technique. In #3 he will concentrate on building a consumer franchise, probably by advertising—a "pull" technique.

Returning to our case discussion of the Harlan Corporation, it next becomes appropriate to ask the students, "Given the importance of the business definition, review the case facts and see if you can deduce the position of Harlan management." Lo and behold, mining was essentially management's point of view, not surprising in a firm that produces basic chemicals. Here was a group of executives inculcated in commodity marketing. Almost automatically they transplanted their basic instincts to the new business.

THE FATAL DANGER, AND HOW TO AVOID IT

So what? Can't a business manager, given a choice of definitions, select any one he wants? Unfortunately not, because one of the three is guaranteed to produce failure for Harlan. Which one?

At first blush it may seem that the far right, the consumer option, is the deadly one. After all, the risks are extremely high in the consumer markets, particularly for a commodity processor. The stereotypical chemical house is likely to fall short in the unfamiliar world of consumer marketing. But not necessarily. The risks may indeed be high, but the outcome is not certain. DuPont did a memorable job with nylon when it concentrated upon the "better end product" (e.g., hosiery) position. Alcoa introduced, and still sells, aluminum pots and pans as well as household foil. The consumer orientation, however, is not without its perils. The path is strewn with the bones of unsuccessful entrants— Kaiser in aluminum foil for the household, Crown Zellerbach in paper diapers, several large banks in retail banking, and DuPont in Corfam.

Guaranteed failure rests in the first column, the commodity alternative. To successfully sell a commodity presupposes an existing demand. Buyers have to know what to do with the product before they will purchase in quantities. Imagine you are a lettuce salesman for the Bruce Church Company; you call one of your supermarket buyers and try to sell a carload of lettuce, and he asks, "What's lettuce?"

The commodity, or hardware, definition is the only one that is not viable in entirely new product launches. Harlan management, because they fell into that unhappy choice, did most things wrong—as if they were selling a well-recognized, mature product.

Some further reflections about the three-way definitional choice for Harlan—"mining," "tile manufacturer," or "better end products"— suggest that the three alternatives are reflective of our old conceptual friend, the product life cycle from specialty to commodity, but drawn backward:

Commodity $\longleftarrow$ Specialty

The innovator can launch from the right or from the center, but not from the left. Most industrial firms probably prefer to enter from the center—the end user markets call for "foreign" skills. Consider Texas Instruments trying to crack the consumer market for personal computers.

All of this leads to another speculation: might not the preferred strategy be to select a particular viable column (or definition), develop some know-how, and stay with it? Why, for example, switch intermittently from one market orientation to another? Why not become a specialist in terms of customers or consumers?

That's not so easy to do, unfortunately, and for two reasons: (1) If the business definitions essentially parallel the product life cycle, there will be an inevitable drift toward the left, modified, to be sure, by the firm's ability to "turn the arrow." (2) A multiproduct company will have products in each column, at any one moment of time. Hence the marketing manager has to be adept at handling a mix of strategies. For some items the manager needs a specialty marketing approach, for others an ability to work with original equipment manufacturers (OEMs), for still others the ability to move commodities. If the manager really wants to concentrate on only one approach, there is usually only a single choice, the commodity extreme.

This constant evolution of strategic requirements poses a serious management problem—change seems simple, but in practice it is difficult to execute. In fact, it is so difficult that most companies can't continuously pull it off and as a result have reasonable short market lives. Just count the survivors from a list fifty years ago of the five hundred largest companies.

Constant adaptation calls for more flexibility than most organizations can muster. The problem shows up today in an interesting way: whereas we talked considerably during the 1970s about "strategic planning," we now talk about "implementation."

What good is a strategic plan if the real obstacle is how to obtain employees' commitment as well as their understanding of the new strategic requirements? There has been over the years a noticeable shift from ad hoc action, to one-year budgets, to forecasts, to long-range planning, to strategic market planning, and now to implementation.

Implementation of new strategies is a difficult management challenge because it is complex and includes a number of tough organizational issues. At one large contract feeding and restaurant company, for example, top management decided, for compelling reasons, to reorient middle management toward a marketing point of view. The company's whole tradition had been excellence in operations, in which respect the firm truly excelled. Local management's orientation naturally was operations—so much so that individual managers reactively inspected their units by walking in through the kitchen door. It never occurred to them to walk in through the front door. A front door, or consumer, orientation was therefore senior management's change objective. In order to guarantee rapid acceptance among the operating managers, the executives commissioned a well-respected consulting firm to analyze each unit's marketing opportunities and to recommend programs of action. Over a one-year period the consultants made their investigation and submitted an impressive report. It was a year later that top management decided to check what recommended changes had actually been implemented.

Unfortunately the answer was none. The company still had a closet filled with recommendations (the equivalent of a strategic plan), but field behavior was as it always had been. The kitchen door prevailed. What went wrong? A special marketing committee hypothesized the reasons and concluded that in order to reorient the personnel, seven steps should have been taken:

1. Get their attention; that is, make sure that the critical individuals will listen to new ideas.

2. Make an analysis and recommendations—the task of the consultants.

3. Earn the employees' commitment to the new plan. Do they understand and feel involved?

4. Train the people to perform the new tasks. Just because the preferred behavior is spelled out, that is no assurance that the managers can or will do it that way.

5. Restructure all of the jobs for two reasons: (1) because managers have no idle time and if the senior executives want new marketing actions, they must relieve the operating people of specific operating tasks; (2) to prevent managers who adopt the new suggestions from being punished within the organization—and there are many ways organizations can punish the deviant.

6. Establish an evaluation and reward system that reinforces the new behavior.

7. Set up a control and feedback mechanism so that management can monitor progress.

The reader may well find these seven steps incomplete, but it is nonetheless useful to ask, Which of these steps is the easiest to perform? Which the hardest?

Most observers will agree that step 2—the consultant's report—is the easiest. All it takes is sufficient money to pay the fees. The other steps have varying degrees of complication. Step 1, getting their attention, is hardly simple. Nor is training, establishing a control system, assuring commitment, or providing incentives. Perhaps the biggest problem lies, however, with the job restructuring. This probably means gutting the organization in the sense of drastically altering the culture.

To reorient an organization, we conclude, is not simple. Nonetheless, successful companies do manage to address particular environmental problems and opportunities. When the match between management's strengths and the outside opportunities is good, the strategic window is said to be open. "Run for the roses" under these conditions, for eventually the window will close and management must try again to find a fit. Notwithstanding, adaptation to new environmental requirements is characterized by considerable internal (and external, i.e., competition) resistance. A company may be able to marshal its human resources and reorient them one, two, or even three times, but somewhere the string will run out.

THE NOTION OF KNACKS

In the context of adaptation, companies have knacks or inherent skills. They are most comfortable, to use our earlier illustration, with one or the other of the business definitions. They may have to adapt to several over time, but they still favor one. One of the fundamental problems in any acquisition program is that managements often try to marry dissimilar knacks and then wonder why the presumed synergy fails to materialize.

A company's basic knack is not necessarily obvious. Is Coca-Cola successful because it makes better soft drinks than anyone else, or is its knack one of mass communications? Does a fast-food operator provide superior food, or is its essential knack the management of a franchise system? There is many a high-tech firm today whose knack entails converting an edge of a state-of-the-art idea into a working prototype— which management unfortunately can't market.

Knowing its knack is an essential marketing requirement for the emerging enterprise. The business definition, and the resulting strategy, should reflect the knack. Otherwise there will be trouble. To illustrate, a business friend started an audio tape company and recorded music on tape. During a marketing seminar the president was particularly impressed with a reading of Ted Levitt's "Marketing Myopia." He enthusiastically expounded, "This reading has really opened my eyes. I'm not in the tape business, I'm really in the entertainment business!" Unfortunately he believed this and bought a radio station, a small TV station, and a book publishing company. In 1980, on sales of $30 million, our friend lost $12 million. The "entertainment" additions were his undoing since he couldn't run those diverse units and had to unload them. Recently he was asked what business he was in. Without hesitation he replied, "I make tape!" In a way, all of us "make tape." We need to stick to our essential skills. But that has its potential dangers.

Firms, over time, build up an internal reservoir of competence that is hard to modify. Additionally, they establish, in parallel, a set of beliefs about their world. The beliefs and the competence are self-reinforcing and unfortunately stifle the company's ability to adapt to new requirements.

A student made an interesting observation in this respect. He had just finished a project on how semiconductor companies manage themselves, and he concluded:

> When you reread my interview notes with senior management from the leading companies, it is obvious that these managers share an implicit set of "first principles of management." They believe in the semiconductor business [of that day, 1976], for example, in:
>
> 1. Alacrity—the ability to turn an entire company around rapidly.
> 2. Cost control—due to the problems of low yields and management's belief in the experience curve.
> 3. Technological mastery, particularly the implications of the new technology, e.g., "The microprocessor will revolutionize the way the world lives."
> 4. Vertical integration—it doesn't pay to just make the chips; you must make the calculator and the watch.
> 5. Best people—or someone I have known for twenty years and who came out of Fairchild.

These shared beliefs may be right or they may be wrong. That's immaterial. But they do define the competitive culture for this particular industry. It would be suicidal for a "Harlan Chemical," with its own shared beliefs, to compete or acquire in this different world. This is another reason for understanding well your business and your knacks.

ATTRIBUTES OF A GOOD BUSINESS DEFINITION

So much for the importance of defining the business. Are there any suggestions for what makes a good definition?

We know of one that we consider a useful model. During the 1970s, IBM's commercial computer operations described its business this way:

"We solve commercial business problems, by means of computers." That's an interesting and suggestive definition. To be specific, it is couched in terms of the customer's needs, not the manufacturer's hardware. Moreover, it is attainable and, more critical, affects favorably the behavior of the IBM salespeople. A salesman, to illustrate, will surely behave differently if he is solving problems than if he is charged with "selling computers." The impact upon behavior is clear cut: act like a consultant, solve problems!

Dr. Derek Abell suggests in his book on business definitions that a good business definition should satisfy a number of conditions:[3]

Identify the customer group.

Identify the customer need.

Describe the technology.

Define the scope (i.e., how many of each?).

Describe the basis for differentiation.

The IBM definition doesn't meet all of Abell's criteria, but it rates reasonably well. As an additional point it is pertinent to note that Abell's approach never specifies a particular product, but it establishes critical boundaries.

SUMMARY

A statement of the firm's direction is the first prerequisite for marketing strategy. Direction requires specific answers to such questions as What business are we in? Where are we going—the markets, the product areas, the opportunities? What are our goals and objectives?

The answers are fundamental because the marketing strategy will reflect the business definition, whether that definition is explicit or not. Moreover, the business definition will change to reflect the product's position in its life cycle—from specialty to commodity. Over time, strategy shifts, which means that the typical firm must adapt constantly to the changing environment. Unfortunately, such change is difficult to maintain because organizations develop momentum of their own. Hence firms are wisest to identify their basic knack and try to build on that knack for as long as possible. You can't be what you are not.

---

[3] Derek Abell, *Defining the Business: The Starting Point of Strategic Planning* (Englewood Cliffs, N.J.: Prentice-Hall, 1980).

For the emerging company this definitional effort should be a group task—for example, an assignment for the key managers. They will each gain, through the experience, a fuller appreciation for the requirements of the markets as well as develop a spirit of cohesion and team comprehension, which are hard to develop any other way.

4

The Marketing Plan: Analytic or Creative?

There is some generally sound advice in the old saw "Any plan is better than no plan at all." Most of the time that's true, though we can all conjure up a plan so outlandish that the alternative of none is better. But in ordinary circumstances some forethought is better than blind luck.

This doesn't mean, of course, that the forethought, or plan, has to be elaborate. As a matter of fact, that's hardly possible in an emerging company. After all, the marketing manager has no staff and must personally prepare the plan while handling many other responsibilities.

The marketing plan, whatever its form, is pivotal: it is the starting point for the plans of R&D and manufacturing. In a new company this plan may be triggered by the fact that, at long last, there is a product to sell. The question becomes, How many of these can be made? Or it may be that R&D has been given an initial target to produce major competitive improvements and they are now ahead of (or behind) schedule. Such examples are usually the facts of life in a young concern, and the marketing plan must take them into account.

Marketing, because it deals with the customers, has to be the guiding influence. Where should this early limited production be shipped to get the best initial market position, to make the best marketing test for a good future reference, or to obtain the best price? How can we capitalize on an unexpectedly early R&D breakthrough? Or how best can we continue with the present line until R&D catches up? More generally, how can we continue to make our profit targets despite the occurrence of something consequential for which plans could not be made? Those questions will not be answered in the lab, the plant, or the controller's office, but only by the marketing team.

A marketing plan that is assembled seriously, with attainable goals and quotas, with input from below, is an elegant management tool— when management believes in its importance. It will only serve its true purpose if those who formulate it understand clearly that they will be expected to carry it out, and that management incentives, promotions, and recognition will depend upon its prompt execution.

To their advantage, emerging companies can begin market planning without the excess baggage of the mature bureaucratic organization. In this regard it is well to keep in mind two important features of good plans. First, the plan must be recognized as a living document that can, and will, be changed during its life cycle as events dictate. (As one chief executive remarked, "When conditions change, forget the plan and do what's best for the business!")

Second, the plan should contain some contingency measures, the purpose, needless to say, being to minimize the disruption of surprises.

THE FUNDAMENTALS

We began this book by introducing three questions that the emerging enterprise has to consider: (1) Are the market and the product viable? (2) Can we do it? (3) Will the payoff be worthwhile? Positive answers to these queries represent the ultimate test of the marketing (and other) plans, whether written or carried in the manager's head. How, then, do we create such a plan?

There are a number of useful alternatives. We have selected one that is easy and flexible. It is structured around seven building blocks. We have also assumed, because it is a reasonably common time frame, a five-year planning horizon.

1. *Trends.* Because tomorrow's world will be different, we start by speculating about the new world. What will it be like in five years? What are the important trends that will shape that environment? We don't, of course, speculate about the "entire world"—that would be a never-ending task better left to philosophers. We are interested in our own little corner, today's business.

   Most of the trends are reasonably easy to identify (e.g., "The market will continue to grow by 25 percent," "Rationalization of the industry will accelerate and large firms will absorb small ones," "The new technology will be launched in this time frame"). From a practical point of view, the process of trend identification can be simplified if the manager separates the trends into categories, such as customers, competitors, technology, channels of distribution, political climate, and the state of the economy.

Where does the manager find this information? Everywhere. Sometimes in books and articles (such as population projections) and sometimes in conversation with colleagues, customers, competitors, and industry experts. Managers are typically willing to share their views about the future; after all, tomorrow is a critical period for all of us.

2. *Problems and Opportunities.* Once the trends are gathered, we can begin to isolate tomorrow's problems and opportunities. Unless the problems, which are scattered among the trends, are overcome, the five-year plan will be useless. Problems serve as the ultimate check of our intended strategy.

Now for the good news: we turn the coin over and search for opportunities. What is an opportunity? It may be a crude definition, but an opportunity is "any way to make a buck." Opportunities, quite clearly, spell out the growth and profit possibilities and, in turn, are derived from the trends. In many cases, in fact, opportunities are suggested by a problem; for example, "If we re-engineer the adapter, we might avoid a direct confrontation with the giant competitor and find instead a nice specialty niche."

Because opportunities come in many shapes and sizes, any collection that we deduce from the trends will not be totally compatible internally. A company can't be large and small at the same time, any more than it can be general and specific. And yet each of these characteristics may represent potentials for profit. So it's useful to subdivide our opportunities into compatible sets. We may not want to pursue all the possibilities in any one set, but at least we could. This sorting permits us to choose one or more sets, using whatever criteria make economic sense.

3. *Business Definition.* Our selected opportunity set is pure and simply tomorrow's business definition. After all, if a business definition isn't made up of opportunities, what good is it? As one would anticipate, this definition of tomorrow's business is unlikely to differ much from our "going-in definition"—that is, unless the

trends and opportunities are radically changed from today. Such drastic change would be uncommon.

4. *Critical Success Factors.* Armed with our new business definition, we must now ask, What will we have to be good at to succeed in this business? What are the critical success factors? We ask this question for an obvious reason: do we appreciate the implications of the new direction? It follows, moreover, that the CSFs will define the arena within which tomorrow's strategy must be executed.

5. *Alternative Strategies.* Too often managers select their strategy from an inadequate list of other possibilities. They stick with the familiar. To minimize that danger it is appropriate at this point to single out as many different marketing strategies as possible that are compatible with tomorrow's business. How many ways can we think of to skin the cat? After all, one might use a direct or indirect distribution approach, a push or pull communication strategy, a penetration or a skimming price technique, an innovative or a follower product development policy.

6. *The Current Marketing Strategy.* Among other things, we have now identified external threats and opportunities as well as proposed marketing approaches. But can we make it all work? Are we able to execute the new business? To help answer this critical question, we need to take a close look at our own strengths and weaknesses. A handy way to structure this analysis is to ask ourselves, "What is our present marketing strategy and why is it what it is?" An honest reply will clearly identify our internal strengths and weaknesses. The question, in addition, permits us to decide whether a continuation of today's strategy will realize our company's long-term goals. If it will, then strategy alternatives are unnecessary, or the business goals should be raised.

7. *A Short-Term (1–2 Years) and a Long-Term (5 Years) Strategy.* Our final step is to match external opportunities with internal strengths, the culmination of the strategic planning process. Normally, this matching provides management with several strategic choices. Some will be short term (one to two years) because the constraints restrict our options. But in five years constraints can be modified, which means alternative five-year possibilities. The final selection will be determined by "pricing out" the alternatives and selecting the most desirable.

The seven steps have been presented as a chronological sequence. However, that's rarely the case in practice. Planning is iterative. You go back and forth until a satisfactory fit is realized (e.g., "I can't select this set of opportunities because my production deficiencies are too great!"). Some managers, moreover, like to vary the order of the topics, perhaps introducing step 6 (current strategy) sooner. Notwithstanding, the planning approach described encompasses the major issues that must be considered, either formally or informally.

The plan serves a second purpose: it is the umbrella under which detailed financial plans can be constructed. Forecasts are a case in point.

FORECASTING

Forecasts are the translation of the marketing plan into short-term and long-term sales and cost estimates. Forecasts make it possible for management to size the potential market, to establish quotas and other performance criteria, to predict the manufacturing needs, and to anticipate R&D requirements. Forecasts are essentially how we compare the profitability of various marketing plans. "Is it more profitable to go with plan A or plan B?" "Which product lines, from a profit and loss point of view, should we add? Which should we drop?"

It is helpful, at the outset, to consider some of the attributes of good forecasts. Many managers over the years have favored the following "truisms":

1. A "bottoms-up" approach is better than top management dictation. Field people, ours or independent middlemen, need to be involved. Additionally, without their input, forecasts will be sterile and lacking in the nuances of the marketplace. At the same time, there must be a fudge factor in the final plan that allows for local subjectivity.

2. Forecasts that are at odds with other long-range expectations need to be reexamined, and the variance identified.

3. Forecasts must be taken seriously because they are a fundamental management tool. Until a better substitute appears, they represent the backbone of the management control system.

4. The basic field data should be validated by the successive judgments of the management hierarchy. For example, at Memorex regional phone calls are made each week to each branch after receipt of that week's "90 Day Rolling" forecast by each of thirty-two salesmen,

working out of six branch offices. The regional manager personally reviews each forecast and compares it with the previous week's, not only to establish validity but to determine what has happened to those accounts that have disappeared or not added as new prospects.

5. The forecaster must maintain a continuous dialogue with marketing management to include in the estimate allowances for changes in the mix.

In terms of "how to forecast," there are six operating techniques in common use which, in turn, can be grouped into three major categories: what people say, what people do, and what people have done.

What People Say

Modified by cost constraints as well as data availability and reliability, this research approach consists of three operating techniques: surveys of buyer intentions, composite of sales force opinions, and expert opinions.

The value of buyer intentions depends largely upon the extent to which the buyers have clearly formulated intentions and will carry them out. Buyer-intention surveys have proven to be particularly useful in the purchase of major consumer durables, as well as industrial goods.

The appropriateness of sales force opinions increases to the extent that (a) sales representatives are likely to be the company's most knowledgeable source of grass-roots information; (b) sales representatives are cooperative; (c) their views are unbiased or their biases can be corrected; and (d) there are some side benefits, such as encouraging better estimating from the field.

Finally, by tapping the opinions of well-informed people (such as distributors or outside experts), a manager can realize forecasts quickly and cheaply, and with a different, perhaps more objective, viewpoint than those of his or her compatriots. However, this method is usually more reliable for aggregate forecasting than for developing accurate breakdowns by territory, customer group, or product.

What People Do

The standard technique in this category is the market test, which is especially desirable when forecasting the sales of a new product or the likely sales of an established product in a new channel or territory. The objective is to obtain representative results by experimenting in a small piece of the market.

What People Have Done

Finally, there is the approach of reviewing history—what have people done? The first technique is that of time-series analysis, which assumes a pattern over time. Yesterday's sales, in other words, are extrapolated to predict future sales. Extrapolation is sometimes a reliable technique and sometimes not; it assumes, unfortunately, regularity over time.

Statistical demand analyses, on the other hand, depend upon determining which independent variables best explain the variation in the sales of the target product. How these variables might move in the future can then be predicted and applied to the specific product. Tire sales, to be obvious, are a function of auto sales.

Despite the seeming accuracy of these technical procedures, the manager must temper his conclusions with an interpretation of the environmental influences. He must take into account all kinds of possibilities—changes in demography, segment income, price indices, technology, competitive products, general economics, political temper, and fiscal policies. The reader will readily understand that many of these influences are hard to quantify.

We have implied tacitly, in our remarks to date, that our plans and forecasts are meant to cover domestic markets only. We don't wish to leave that impression because "U.S. only" would be a serious error. International markets are usually well worth pursuing for the emerging enterprise. We shall include, therefore, some explicit comments about the export markets and how to pursue them.

INTERNATIONAL MARKETING

Managers in many emerging companies overlook the export markets for a variety of reasons:

- They have no time.
- They are unfamiliar with foreign customs, languages, and laws.
- They foresee high costs and risks.
- They are too apathetic to get involved in the necessary planning, organization, and product adjustments.

Their inaction can be expensive. Selling overseas often provides a 25 or 30 percent increase in volume, with attractive cash flows and superior margins. And there is recent legislation, the Export Trade Act, which facilitates foreign business. The act provides a whole set of new opportunities for bank financing and an incentive for banks to take an active interest in the emerging company's financial affairs. The act provides that banks, for the first time, may actually invest in export trading companies. It is designed particularly to help the new young company that finds it difficult to obtain inventory and receivables financing, by authorizing the Export-Import Bank to guarantee such loans under a broad range of circumstances previously excluded.

Nor can unfamiliarity be a legitimate reason for avoiding overseas opportunities. There are export trading companies that provide all the necessary services between suppliers and their overseas markets. It is therefore not necessary for the CEO or other key executives to personally take on the time-consuming task of starting an international business.

There are, of course, a few caveats that one should be aware of. In order to do business overseas, or internationally, it is not necessary to be everywhere. Going to Europe with a product does not mean fourteen countries. In fact, it might very well simply mean selling through a good channel in one, such as France, England, or Germany. The worst thing to do is hire some individual who speaks good English (this automatically means he is smart to many American executives) and let him set you up (read that as you wish) in all of Latin America or Europe.

In choosing distributors or dealers, remember that the early negotiations are usually crucial and have a lasting effect. Try not to give exclusivity for an entire country to one firm. If this cannot be avoided, then at least protect yourself by a clause that ties these exclusive rights to meeting a quarterly set of sales goals as well as prompt payments. These simple safeguards allow you later, if the dealer falls short, to simply appoint one or more additional ones and avoid legal trouble by leaving the dealer as is. Try to deal in FOB American dollars secured through the dealer's bank by a letter of credit or bank draft guarantee. You may wish to begin with an open account system in a gesture of friendship, but it is much wiser to be seriously businesslike at the outset. Dealing in dollars simply protects you from surprise losses due to currency fluctuation, and is a prudent step. FOB the U.S. means that the dealer handles customs, duty, and freight, which are items of some intricacy for the uninitiated. On the other hand, if the only way in which someone will handle your product is CIF, and in French francs, it is relatively simple to obtain an experienced foreign trade administrator. Just because the rules are different does not mean the entire subject is arcane or a black art.

If advertising is an important part of your product sale, it is usually sound practice to grant a matching allowance and let the local people determine what agency and media to use. It really is true that *color* is spelled *colour* in the United Kingdom, and that the metric system is used throughout the Western world except the United States, and that American slang slogans are often offensive. At least in the beginning, turn that part over to those who know best and for whom the consequences of error are most severe, your local dealer.

Translations of spec sheets, customer information bulletins, and operating instructions are tricky. First, don't prepare them in the United States, and second, don't rely totally on the local secretary, or friend of the dealer, to take on this vital task unsupervised. Always have the translated draft carefully reviewed by a professional translator.

When dealing with foreign business people, remember that many of them have "two-thousand-word Berlitz English" vocabularies. They do not speak sophisticated English any more than most Americans speak fluent French or German. Avoid slang expressions, confirm in short, well-written telexes your phone conversations, and practice redundancy in your conversations. Whenever possible, express in two different ways any really important point. If you are not sure what has or has not been understood, it is perfectly appropriate to inquire whether it is clear, and suggest that the listener give you an example of what you mean.

Finally, when you visit your distributors, try not to do the five-country, seven-day, typically American swing around the territory. Leave enough time to listen, observe, and respond; it really can make an important difference, and frequently you will return with a good marketing idea for the United States as well.

Don't disregard the very extensive helping hand offered by the U.S. Department of Commerce. They have an excellent library, lots of first-rate publications, and many experienced people who are eager to help young and old companies pursue international trade. They will, for example, recommend distribution channels and help check the credit and business worthiness of alternative agents, as well as assist with trade fairs and appropriate introductions to foreign business contacts. It is not necessary to go to Washington for this help since the Commerce

Department has field offices in most major U.S. cities and at all U.S. embassies. In the event that your products are subject to export control, it is essential that you make arrangements immediately to obtain the department's help, which tends to be largely unbureaucratic.

The message is: Look overseas early for a profitable source of increased business.

PLANNING OR OPPORTUNISM?

We want to emphasize, at this point, the absolute need to be sensible about planning. It's all too easy to go overboard and substitute, in the preparation, form for substance. Many a large company displays with pride its weighty planning book but carefully overlooks the fact that it is seldom used, or that it has become a straitjacket. The desire in these companies for uniformity among their plans has sadly resulted in standardized techniques and sterile programs.

The need, it follows, is for balance and a "reasonable point of view." Precision and completeness are ideals that can never be realized in planning. This state of affairs becomes clearer if we revert to something mentioned earlier. Marketing, according to one of our definitions, provides the general manager with direction, strategy, and the completed sale. The order of these three is not casual, and it's important that you take note of their sequencing in your company. The sequence reflects crucial differences in management style. To illustrate:

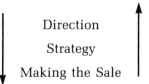

Direction

Strategy

Making the Sale

The arrows are meant to indicate different management approaches. To the left—the "planning" mode—the decision process is to decide initially what business you are in and where you hope to go and then to deduce the strategy and sales requirements. To the right, the firm's momentum follows the sales leads. It chases the opportunities. The first smacks of purpose, the second of reaction or opportunism. Which is better?

The answer, not surprisingly, is both. Planning promises order and control—it holds out the hope for a peaceful, regulated life—but it rests its promise entirely on the planner's ability to predict the future, a wishful thought at best. How many significant business events have you ever predicted? How many business-affecting influences have you foreseen? No one can predict. A plan is nothing more than the composite of many assumptions about tomorrow. It rests, very often, upon an extrapolation of what has occurred, a dubious foundation, given our fast-moving markets. Notwithstanding, and despite these reservations, the exercise of planning has one overriding virtue: it forces management to consider seriously the possibilities and to reappraise periodically its traditional assumptions.

The bottom-to-top sequence (the right side of our little diagram) is primarily opportunistic. Direction follows from the situation, and that's not all bad. Many emerging enterprises depend for their survival upon a prompt response to external conditions. They make out because they can move in on opportunities with alacrity. Their risk, unfortunately, is that they may never latch on to a healthy long-term trend but rather may drift from point to point essentially dependent upon spontaneous circumstances. Or they may scatter their limited resources. A combination of each extreme's strong points would therefore seem a sensible compromise for the manager.

The balance between the left and right has shifted over the years. During the 1960s and '70s managers developed increasing reliance upon planning. This reliance reflects essentially an analytic orientation. Managers, during these years, peppered their vocabulary with such buzz words as *long range and strategic planning, experience curves,* and *product portfolios.* Unfortunately, there was a price for all this rigor: inflexibility, staff domination, paperwork, and technique-worship. It was less "what you do" than "how you do it." Implementation was separated from planning. The result was not surprising: many elaborate plans were left unused. Missing from the calculations was the willingness and ability of the line managers to carry out the strategic recommendations. The constraints of the corporate culture, it seems, were more powerful than the analytic reasoning.

For a combination of these reasons, there has been lately a countermovement. Management is redirecting its sights to action, to getting things done. Companies seem increasingly to assign planning to their line operators where the link between planning and implementation is direct (and short). Immediate response to the changing environment becomes the treasured ability. An amusing but also revealing little story illustrates this change of heart. One of the writers was asked to deliver a talk called "Strategic Market Planning." As the presentation day neared, it became increasingly clear to the speaker that the exact meaning of the title was not self-evident. Is there, for example, an opposite expression, "Nonstrategic Market Planning"? Or even "Strategic Market Implementation"? By chance, the speaker had lunch with a successful president whose firm had been growing at a healthy clip, and he asked, "What do you think *strategic market planning* means?" "I don't know," was the president's reply, "but I sure hope my competitors do it!" The implications are clear. Undue analysis and system will cut into the firm's ability to react rapidly.

Incidentally, the popularity of the microcomputer should speed this trend toward line planning and execution and further relieve the marketing manager of staff dependence. Now the manager can do his own "what if" modeling at his desk without major data processing equipment and programming resources. All kinds of information are within arm's length, and there is a pyramiding supply of software that permits analysis, comparison, and graphic display. In respect to field forecasts, for instance, personal computers provide the opportunity for prompt comparisons with previous forecasts as well as the opportunity to observe quickly the results of changes in strategy or product mix.

The melding of planning and execution at the operating level should be healthy. It will supplement, one hopes, the earlier reliance by many managements upon cost control as the preferred approach to profit improvement and introduce some customer creation alternatives. The way to make money is to sell more at a profit, not to close down the Latin American operation or sell off a delinquent department. In short, there is a move toward marketing solutions instead of finance and control.

A PLEA FOR CREATIVITY IN MARKETING

Marketing is a creative function as well as analytic. The balance must be deliberately maintained, especially given the recent management flirtation with the analytic.

It is not simple to write dispassionately about creativity and analysis. In the first place, the words conjure up all kinds of images and emotions. Artists scorn analysts as routine and uninspiring clods, while the hard thinkers dismiss the creative as softheaded and ethereal. There are, moreover, puzzling definitional problems having to do with "degree" of creativity and analysis. What is creative to a marketing manager is not likely to be creative to Leonardo da Vinci or Michelangelo. What is analytic to the sales manager would be viewed as insignificant by the nuclear physicist. Marketing strategies, in more cases than not, are made up of both creativity and analysis and can't therefore be labeled as all one or the other.

Nonetheless, it is useful to recognize that analytic is the opposite of creative; they are not two sides of the same coin. Deductive is not inductive. Hence, the manager must strive continuously to intermingle them. The analyst without creativity is a "number cruncher"; the dancer without system would twirl around uncontrollably or fall on her face.

Creativity in marketing spawns alternative (and better) solutions. It revels in the unexpected, the novel. It is the solution that springs from a burst of inspiration, rather than from an inch-by-inch deductive crawl.

Professor Theodore Levitt at Harvard distinguishes creativity from innovation. He contends that business suffers not from a lack of creativity, but rather from too little innovation. He defines innovation as the translation of creativity into action. Nor is this an automatic process. Quite the contrary. It is a well-acknowledged management principle that a new idea will succeed only if there is a champion to run with it.

The analytic approach has dominated management thinking in business, and education, since the 1960s. Most MBA programs stress deduction—statistics, operations research, strategic planning, financial analysis. Management has been treated too often as "a bag of tools and techniques."

The ascendancy of the analytic approach has been particularly hard on marketing, which is essentially a creative phenomenon. Marketing depends for its internal logic upon the theory of buying behavior. But there is no single theory of buying behavior. Rather there are many, such as utility theory, cognitive dissonance, conditioned response, Freudian, group behavior, and so on. All kinds of social scientists are engaged in this behavioral investigation, including personnel psychologists, perception psychologists, human biologists, sociologists, and economists. The result is a mosaic of theories as diverse as the results of a committee trying to describe an elephant. We have no overriding set of principles.

What does this all mean to the marketing practitioner? Without a general theory of behavior, he's not sure why behavior occurs—causation is not clear. Hence pragmatism is the only reasonable approach. Instead of theory, the manager essentially works with "currently useful generalizations." His is an experimental approach. He depends largely upon observation, common sense, and intuition. He is more related to the inductive, creative artist than to the rationalist. All of this means that marketing has a different orientation than, say, finance, operations research, or accounting—all much more structured subjects. Consider this dichotomy of values:

FINANCE AND OPERATIONS RESEARCH	MARKETING AND SALES MANAGEMENT
Deductive	Inductive
Analytic	Creative
Model or theory	Facts
Causation	Inspiration

Can you conjure up the conversation that goes on between analyst and marketing executive in the typical company? The president/analyst says to the marketer, "I'd be glad to release the $500,000 for your new project if you'd just answer a few simple questions. How many of these new products are you going to sell by model number, color, design, and days of the week in the various parts of the market?" The marketing manager's response is classic: "Don't worry about it!" And, if the manager wants to be quantitative, "We're going to sell a lot!"

We shouldn't be too flippant about the contrasts in language between the two philosophic approaches. But the reality is that marketing people do have different values; they do talk a different language. Marketing purists typically believe in seniority ("It takes time to develop judgment and experience"), whereas analysts are no respecters of age ("If you're not making good decisions by the time you are twenty-five, you'll never make them!"). Contrast the normal age of a sales manager with a product manager. There's probably a ten-year difference!

We can hardly settle in a few pages this age-old conflict between the deductive thinker and the inductive. We do know, of course, that the pendulum has been swinging back and forth for centuries. In the United States, at present, there is a substantial reawakening of interest in the humanitarian dimensions of management, including quality circles, matrix organizations, the "corporate culture," and collaborative decision making. For marketing managers there is beginning to be reconfirmation of what they have always instinctively known: the quantitative by itself is not the answer.

SUMMARY

Companies usually grow by a combination of planning and opportunism. Planning helps to introduce order, but it rests upon our ability to forecast. Opportunism allows us to capture unexpected bonanzas as they arise. We have tended, in American management, to overstress the analytic. But the fact is that marketing managers must temper their planning desires with the limitations of predicting. Probably the best that we can expect from a formal planning procedure is to anticipate those events that will probably follow from the recent past, to identify our critical assumptions and judgments, to entertain options, and to teach our managers to think about alternatives.

Sound planning follows a seven-step process. Specific to any plan are the forecasts of sales and expenses. Marketing managers use a range of forecasting approaches, most of which are essentially common sense.

Our most serious current deficiency in marketing is creativity. Creativity is particularly relevant to the marketing executive, who doesn't have the luxury of a theoretical base to permit heavy reliance upon deduction.

5

Marketing Strategy: The Basics

WHAT IS STRATEGY?

Marketing strategy is the blueprint by which the enterprise intends to realize its marketing objectives, be they sales, profits, or market share. A few examples are useful for illustrating the nature of effective strategies—their common elements, their characteristics, and their evolution.[1]

Versatec Five years after its founding, Versatec was the leader in the rapidly growing electrostatic (nonimpact) printing field. Instead of concentrating on maximizing machine speed, as most of its competitors had chosen to do, Versatec designed a less costly product that printed only 1,000 characters per second (still faster than most output devices); used modular construction and interchangeable parts; targeted the printers at the small computer and OEM research markets; priced the machines at one half the competitive level (with a gross margin of 50 percent); sold the printers through exclusive representatives (rather than company salespeople); and restricted marketing communications to trade shows, technical literature, and customer brochures.

Casio Between 1970 and 1980 Casio emerged as the world's largest producer of digital watches and hand-held calculators. During this ten-year period, sales jumped from $30 million to $700 million. Casio's success was largely due to a marketing strategy that called for low prices and the development of innovative features.

In 1981, however, Casio's sales and profits leveled out for the first time. Company executives felt that this break in growth was permanent

---

[1] These examples were drawn from a Stanford Graduate School of Business teaching case, *The Meriden Company* (S-M 169R) Revised 1984.

in that the world market for digital watches and calculators had become saturated. To regain momentum, Casio executives diversified and added two new product lines: electrical musical instruments and personal computers. Realizing that the company's low-price image was not appropriate for these products, Casio executives drastically altered their communication strategy. As one Casio official states, "The Casio image during the 1970s was not associated with the purchase of electric musical equipment or personal computers, both of which require much time and energy to buy." Casio's new marketing strategy called for relying more on quality and innovation than on price and innovation. Subsequent to Casio's new strategy, it positioned all of its products, including its digital watches and hand-held calculators, as quality items in the moderate to high price range.

Pillsbury—Funny Face Until Funny Face (a drink mix for kids), Pillsbury was mostly involved in flour and baking. The introduction of Funny Face entailed an entirely new approach, both to the market and to top management.

As to the market, Pillsbury began with the discovery that its Sweet 10, an artificial sweetener, was being used by some mothers instead of sugar to sweeten Kool-Aid, a competitor's product. Pillsbury's thinking progressed through various stages until it decided to market its own drink mix with the premeasured sweetener already included. The early strategy sessions, however, were nearsightedly focused on the same issue as that of the competition—selling a drink mix to mothers for their children.

Finally, Pillsbury broke through the well-entrenched position of Kool-Aid by deciding to merchandise, not a drink mix, but *fun*. All marketing efforts were then brought into line with this concept; in particular, the strategy would be aimed at selling to kids, not their mothers. Instead of practical pictures of pitchers on the envelope, Pillsbury executives struck on the plan (using their own kids as ideamen) of putting funny-faced oranges, apples, and the like, on the packages. In line with the basic concept, the Pillsbury name was de-emphasized, and Sweet 10 as an ingredient was also played down. Both of these decisions involved risks and moved substantially away from the original plan, which was to build business for the sweetener— in other words, a manufacturing, product-oriented approach. But Funny Face came through and provided a new base for launching other nonflour products.

As a result of its experience with Funny Face, Pillsbury freed its new products people from individual division relationships, forming an entirely new group, directly responsible to the president. Thus their vision is not limited to the particular processes or products of any one division, but is free to move in any direction.

What is common about these three strategies?

Each depicts the underlying logic, but not the tactical details, of how the firm expects to compete. They are, furthermore, long-term, not short-term, in implication. And each has something to say about the key elements in a marketing strategy:

1. The product: its definition, its positioning, its dimensions.
2. The markets: Who are the target audiences? What are their critical needs? What are their alternatives?
3. The price: What is the relative value of the offer vis-à-vis alternatives?
4. The distribution system: How will the product be brought to the user?
5. The communication system: How will the potential buyer be made aware, be induced to try, and persuaded to repurchase?

It is also significant to note, as we stated in Chapter 1, that successful strategies provide the enterprise with a competitive edge. They give the consumer reasons to buy from you and not from the other guy.

Strategy by itself is no guarantee of success because execution may be faulty or the tactics poorly selected. There are many operating tactics available, needless to say. For example, mass media advertising can take the form of TV, radio, magazines, or newspapers; frequent or infrequent insertions; different appeals and visual formats; or local versus national coverage. Tactics normally change frequently, whereas strategy perseveres until there are meaningful shifts in the environment. It is important, of course, that strategy not be inflexibly viewed as "God-given." Every strategy is based upon assumptions that may change unexpectedly. Contingency planning is consequently a sensible adjunct of marketing strategy. The extent to which a variety of alternatives is studied in advance reduces the possibility of surprise. Contingency strategy is often the difference between success and failure.

It is unrealistic to consider marketing strategy by itself. It is but one dimension of a larger process called business planning and thus dependent on the corporate mission and goals as well as its expected interactions with the other business functions (marketing can hardly build a specialty strategy when R&D is process-oriented!). Moreover, as we just noted, marketing strategy depends for its robustness upon effective tactics and execution.

To better appreciate the ramifications of effective strategy we need to delve deeper into the subject than the three brief examples permit. We should consider such issues as how strategies are assembled, the modifications required over time, the effect of market share and market position, and the importance of segmentation.

PRODUCT STRATEGY

Products can be described from a number of points of view, each of which provides meaningful inputs. We have singled out four, one technical and three market-driven.

The engineer, to consider the first, is preoccupied with product specifications, such as one might rely on when buying a computer or an electronic PBX. For a variety of technical purposes such an inventory of engineering attributes is invaluable—in assessing the versatility or range of an instrument, the supply and maintenance requirements of a new turbine, or the complexities and training problems involved in a software program. Products and parts, as we all know, are assembled from such specifications.

But technical descriptions have marketing limitations. Few buyers purchase because they want only the physical attributes. Rather, they seek what the product or service can do for them. The benefits and utilities are what make the product valuable. People don't buy their family home because they want wood, brick, and metal—rather the buyer wants comfort, prestige, substance, and convenience. From a marketing point of view the values are considerably more significant than the specifications. A product, after all, must solve a problem! Unfortunately the industrial world is filled with "nonproducts"—great specifications, but no buyer. A nonproduct is something that works but no one buys it, such as the expensive solution to an inexpensive problem, or the elegant answer to a marginal problem. In other words, there are no meaningful values attached to a nonproduct—only technical characteristics.

All of this means that the definition of a product can be a very tenuous affair. Is a soft drink a sweet-flavored beverage, a respite in an otherwise busy day, the basis for a social interchange, or a mix for a highball? Clearly, these definitional alternatives reflect differences in values or benefits sought. Even more important, and we'll add more to these comments later, any marketing strategy is fully dependent upon the product definition. (Incidentally, it should be clear by now that product definition and business definition are interrelated.)

Product strategy has still another dimension, which we label *positioning*. How, for example, do the customers perceive your product? Is that how management defines it? Are you seen as "the Cadillac of the industry," "the standard," the "low-cost alternative," or what?

An illustration will help. In 1966, Head Skis was beginning to lose momentum while competition was gaining ground. The underlying explanation was that the core markets were beginning to shift, from an emphasis on "the best" skis to "the most stylish." The hard-core skier was being supplemented by the participant who was equally interested in the social amenities of a weekend in the snow. Skiing was suddenly a "mass"-consumption social activity whose participants had a new set of style requirements. This market can be meaningfully mapped in two dimensions, as shown in Figure 5.1.

The hard reality was that Head was isolated in the Exclusive/Functional space while competition was beginning to shift into the other quadrants; the buying public, of course, was the cause of this shift. Head was in trouble, not because it was in the upper right corner, but because that corner was losing its clientele.

A perceptual map is a handy tool for the manager of the emerging company and sparks any number of meaningful queries: (1) Which segment(s) are best suited to our abilities? (2) Which segment(s) have which competitors, and which of these am I willing to tackle? (3) Do I build my offenses with a single product, or do I try several in an attempt to attract different segments? (4) Can I reposition our service?

Two advertising specialists, Jack Trout and Al Ries, have written

FIGURE 5.1

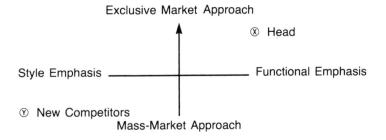

that American advertising progressed from a concentration upon features and benefits ("the unique selling proposition") in the 1950s, to images (the "Marlboro man") in the 1960s, to positioning in the 1970s.[2] Hence the public has recently been exposed to "Seven-Up, the uncola," "When you're out of Schlitz, you're out of beer," and "Caterpillar means twenty-four-hour service."

Finally, we often find it meaningful to talk about a product as a part of a portfolio of products. Just as investment portfolios contain a collection of financial instruments that are separately selected for dozens of reasons (cash flow, entrée into a new field, a competitive weapon, a fast growth possibility, a minimum risk), so, too, should the company's collection of products be assembled. Each product has its own reason for being carried, though the entire line should meet some overall objective (such as "20% ROI" or "50% share of market").

The conclusion? Neither new products nor new markets should be selected for a common set of criteria, such as an "ROI of 15%." Each must supply its own defense and be separately evaluated. These portfolio decisions are particularly sensitive for the emerging company.

SEGMENTATION STRATEGY

Product and segment are inseparable and should almost be treated as Siamese twins. What may be a product to one group of customers (with similar needs) may be a nonproduct to another. The same product or service can have different intensities of attraction for different buyers. Or the same buyer may purchase differently at times, depending upon his or her immediate motivation. Contrast the books you would buy: to read on the airplane; for your child's surprise present; for your spouse's birthday; to display on the end table in your living room. One of the complications of working with segmented markets is that the segments are not always easy to isolate. Notice in the instance above that the book purchaser will be in any of several markets depending upon his or her motivation at that moment.

How do we define a segment? It is any group of consumers whose reaction to a given marketing stimulus is the same. It follows that there is homogeneity within segments but heterogeneity between them. Moreover, in order to be economically useful, a segment must be

---

[2] Jack Trout and Al Ries, "The Positioning Era," *Advertising Age*, April 24, May 1, and May 8, 1972, Crain Communications, Inc.

reachable by some kind of communication medium and it must be large enough to warrant seller effort.

There are several descriptors that practitioners have found useful for segmenting markets, including demography (population dispersal, age, sex); income, race, religion, and education; benefits or values desired (those who want sporty cars as opposed to those who want economical driving); life-style (the swingers versus the savers); the application (do-it-yourself versus professional handymen); heavy users versus light users; and the family life cycle (teenagers versus young marrieds). Remember that the test of these different cross-sectional cuts is their usefulness to the marketing strategist. There is no reason, incidentally, why several cuts might not provide extra insights for the manager: rarely will you find a segment that exactly fits your needs. Nonetheless, devising approximate, sensible segmentation schemes is considerably better than having none whatsoever.

Segmentation is particularly useful in consumer markets where the number of potential buyers is so large that the whole must be broken into manageable parts. The U.S. population, for example, can scarcely be addressed one by one. The industrial markets, on the other hand, are a different story. Customers are limited. For most sales organizations there are maybe 500, 1,500, or 3,000 accounts. Each can be called on separately and treated individually. There is another difference in industrial markets. It is not particularly easy to find meaningful segments. Industrial accounts are complex social and economic organizations that are rarely duplicated. How can one hope to find homogeneous companies? How many Boeings or Lockheeds are there? The most useful basis for segmentation in the industrial world, we conclude, is application or situation.

The practical fact is that the critical "segmenting" instrument in industrial markets is the salesperson. Effective sales individuals are adept at penetrating each of their accounts because they know personally the buyers, the deciders, the influencers, and the "gatekeepers" (e.g., the secretaries).

Segments are significant because they fragment the market into cohesive pieces that the product or sales manager can handle. The manager can adapt his or her marketing strategy to the special needs of each target audience.

The vital connection between strategy and segment can be demonstrated by citing an old but venerable strategy that popped up after World War II. In those postwar years a book publisher, Pocket Books, revolutionized reading habits in the United States by successfully launching the softcover book that we now all take for granted. (Pocket Books was by no means the first in—but it was the first to successfully crack open the mass market.) The firm's strategy, in retrospect, was a lesson in effectiveness:

The Product: Well-known best-sellers or recognized authors; small convenient size; attractive cover; inexpensive material.

The Price: Twenty-five cents, as compared with several dollars for the hardcover alternative.

Distribution: Magazine and newspaper jobbers who received the books on consignment and were given exclusive territories; at retail the books were distributed through thousands of traffic locations that, for a return privilege, displayed the books on special Pocket Book racks placed in easily accessible spots.

Selling: Pocket Books employed its own service sales force, which worked the outlets and reinforced the selling effort of the distributors.

Advertising: There was no advertising program, though individual books contained the titles of other Pocket Book publications.

This market strategy can be summarized as "mass distribution, impulse." It was expensive; certainly the return privilege was not cheap. Nor was the sales and service personnel that kept local displays up to standard. Nevertheless, and after the fact, we know that this strategy succeeded.

But how about "before the fact"? How could Pocket Book management in those days anticipate that theirs was a sensible program? Is there any check that any marketing manager, for that matter, can use to pretest a strategy? There is, and it is contained in two simple questions:

1. If this strategy is to fly, how must the ideal consumer behave?

2. Are there enough of these ideal buyers to make the effort worthwhile?

For Pocket Books we can hypothesize easily that the ideal consumer must be able to read, have twenty-five cents, be mobile, be impulsive, have time on his or her hands, not be interested in shopping, be buying for personal consumption, and be willing to throw the product away.

Given such a buying profile, it follows that the mass-distribution impulse strategy is ideal. (It really has to be, of course, since we derived the profile from the strategy.) All that remains is to "count" the number of such ideal buyers, a task for conventional market research. Strategy, we see, "follows" the segment!

PRICING STRATEGY

Pricing remains one of the most debated and misunderstood marketing activities. Most companies, to make matters worse, don't view pricing as a specialized field, such as they do market research, advertising, and selling. Nor do they typically spend much money on the activity. Not surprisingly, therefore, there are a number of eclectic approaches to the pricing dilemma, four of which are usually mentioned in the literature:

1. Cost plus (which incidentally had the early blessing of the church and political states), in which the marketer adds his desired profit to the costs.

2. Value pricing, or "Charge what the traffic will bear." This logic is rooted in the advantages or benefits gained by the buyer (that is, "How much is our product worth to the customer?").

3. Economic theory, which concludes that price should be set where income from the last unit sold exactly matches costs.

4. Business philosophy, which rejects the economic argument as theoretical, short term, and based upon knowledge impossible to attain. The business approach is to tie price back into the firm's objectives and strategies and recognize that it is finally determined by a wide range of influences, including buyer confidence, stage of the product life cycle, degree of differentiation, demand elasticities, competitive threats, and width and depth of the product line.

Thus it is inconveniently true that a formula approach to pricing is out of the question. There are too many imponderables in the real world that affect the relationships among the pricing determinants. How would the marketing manager, particularly in a new venture, ever guess at the relationship between future sales and prices (the so-called demand curve)? Or further, are sales entirely a function of price, or are promotions, advertising, packaging, and distribution innovations important sales/volume variables?

There are some reasonably standard though empirical approaches that marketers employ. To select one, should the emerging company settle on a penetration or a skimming strategy for the initial price? A wise decision requires that the marketing manager think hard about the essential role of price in his or her overall strategy. What does the manager hope to accomplish with it? To penetrate means to set the initial price so low that rapid sales (and market share) result. The logic of penetration is to secure initial market share and discourage competition.

Penetration pricing entails a number of risks: (1) demand may not be fully responsive to price, so that the innovator "leaves too much money on the table" (i.e., the enterprise could have charged more without losing volume); (2) recovery of the initial investment is postponed, and may never be realized, if technology suddenly changes; (3) a price-cutting atmosphere is established for the industry, which may make profits virtually impossible ever to achieve; (4) cost may not drop as rapidly as the drive for market share assumes.

A skimming strategy is, by way of contrast, quite the reverse—it concentrates on the cream. During his short lead time the innovator takes advantage of the early buyers (who are not price-conscious) and charges what he can get away with. These premium dollars presumably will cover the large investments in R&D and start-up. As the market ages, the seller lowers the price to entice the large, untapped mass of the market.

A skimming strategy has its own perils: (1) large early profits attract hungry competitors, who rush into the market; (2) market penetration is delayed and potential customers may switch to alternative solutions; (3) limited volume prevents the firm from realizing the full economies of scale.

For the emerging company there is always one bedrock consideration that supercedes all the arguments made about skimming or penetrating, namely, the importance of earning a profit. Selling, marketing, moving product into the marketplace, or beating off the competition are of absolutely no value unless they are done for a profit. And unless the marketing department understands this primary responsibility, there will be no cohesive effort to achieve the goals of the emerging company. It is absolutely essential that the chief executive officer insist that marketing management pay attention to profit and not lead him astray on the false assumption that incremental sales can provide incremental profits. In the emerging company this is the nearest thing to disaster.

Each product must stand on its own feet and produce the necessary profit for the planned results of the company.

Some of the more practical insights about pricing have come from research involving behavior (psychology and sociology instead of economics). Such research, not uncommonly, concludes that:

- Industrial buyers are swayed by noneconomic as well as economic influences (homemakers are no less rational than industrial buyers).
- Industrial buyers are characterized by inertia: they do what they did yesterday; they don't like to take chances.
- This conservatism is the result of a lack of confidence in new suppliers: buyers prefer average quality but reliable products over the latest, but least tested, new technology.
- Buyers are willing to pay for confidence (it doesn't make sense for a well-respected market leader to slash prices) but extract a healthy discount if the seller is unknown.

Pricing is largely a trial-and-error process. It is an arena of marketing in which there are consequently any number of "rules of thumb." It is of some interest to note the "principles of pricing" that a group of business executives recently contributed in a class discussion:

1. Use price as a weapon when:
   a. there are no other values or benefits or importance to the buyer
   b. you have excess capacity and can gain incremental volume that will not affect your long-term pricing strategy
   c. you can discourage competition from entering
2. The more competent your sales force, the higher the price you can get.
3. Service is worth money to most customers.
4. Maximum pricing occurs only when you can segment your markets and tackle each segment separately.
5. Price is a function of value or benefits, not of cost.
6. The purpose of the marketing strategy is to avoid competing solely on the basis of price.
7. If you compete on price, be sure you have the most efficient manufacturing facilities.

8. With innovative products, you should be aggressive about pricing; with mature or "me too" products, be prepared for gradual price erosion.

9. It is better to quote a "system price" because you can hide the price of the separate products.

10. System selling is effective when:

    a. you are the recognized leader in some part of the product line

    b. you guarantee a "turnkey" operation to the buyer

11. Demand is much less elastic than you might imagine, owing primarily to inertia and to personal relationships (i.e., past service) between buyer and seller.

12. A salesperson should be judged on the ability to match the product and service to the customer's need. This skill bypasses most price cutting.

13. In today's world, penetration pricing is better than skimming because:

    a. market share is a valuable asset

    b. imitators move too rapidly

    c. you can still skim with a "deluxe model"

14. In a period of inflation, you should raise prices faster than costs— and you can get away with it.

15. It is difficult to manage in a deflation period because it requires tight cost control.

16. Inexperienced managers tend to underprice.

17. Individual product pricing is less important than full-line pricing.

18. In the final analysis, price is usually a less important consideration than might be supposed. Buyers want quality, dependability, assurance of service, technical advice, and attention before they want minimum price.

19. "Cost plus" pricing is reasonable when your developmental expenses are unpredictable and when there is one buyer (such as the military).

20. Price determination should be a compromise between marketing and production, with the balance tilted in favor of marketing.

21. Producers of components are in a weaker pricing position because their products become part of final products.

22. Any idiot can cut prices.

DISTRIBUTION STRATEGY

The fourth element of marketing strategy is that of distribution, or what the buyer has to do to obtain the product and service. It is not a surprise that managers categorize distribution first and foremost as an exercise in logistics—the handling, assembling, storing, and shipping of merchandise. And, indeed, there is a lot to be gained in efficiency and cost reduction by executing the distribution function well. That is why there are so many distributor/retailer specialists.

But distribution, for the creative, can also serve to differentiate the offer. Just contemplate the successful firms that have gained enormous advantages through distribution innovations—McDonald's, self-service grocery stores, L'eggs panty hose, Timex watches (and the use of mass outlets), AT&T (with its telemarketing), communication transporters (with satellites), and the catalog houses. As we have mentioned elsewhere, there is a lot of thought now being directed to the distribution alternatives by the makers of personal computers. The observer of that field can easily spot contrasting examples of distribution approaches: direct mail, catalogs, specialty retailing, manufacturer-owned outlets, OEM sales (to value-added packagers), mass merchandising, discounters, premium houses, leased operations, department stores, and catalog showrooms—to mention only the most obvious. The victory will eventually go to those computer firms that imaginatively cut through the distribution maze.

It is clear that distribution, as a function, is hard to wrap up in neat little packages. There is too much heterogeneity. Wholesaling and retailing can mean different things. How would you label the manufacturer who drop-ships direct to the buyer or even sells on consignment? Or the wholesaler who mail-orders to the ultimate user? Standardized channel definitions are hard to pin down because of the constant changes. Supermarkets now carry many nonfood items, department stores display microcomputers for business markets, discounters carry the most exclusive of designer labels, steel service centers do considerable manufacturing, and industrial manufacturers operate their own retail stores. Traditional merchandise alignments among channels have all but disappeared.

Functionally, at the distributor level, it is traditional to look first at the merchant wholesaler who buys, breaks bulk, finances, inventories, and sells (to retailers or users). These merchant intermediaries stock thousands of items, maintain hundreds of customer contacts and entrées to the dealer markets, and are experts at logistics, but do only a fair to middling job at pioneering new products and markets. Their huge assortment of inventory makes them first and foremost order takers, warehousers, and convenient sources of local inventory.

In a recent article, James Hlavacek and Tommy McCuistion make the case that products with particular attributes are better suited for independent distributors.[3]

1. A large potential customer base (distributors are not specialists)
2. A stockable item that can be serviced locally
3. Small-quantity sales (bulk items normally go direct)
4. Low-level buyer decision, particularly of standard parts
5. Buyer need for fast delivery and service

Tangential to these full-line wholesalers is a group of specialty wholesalers who restrict their operations to selected lines, certain functions, or selected suppliers. As specialists they can offer more aggressive marketing programs.

Next there is a host of specialist middlemen who don't stock, such as brokers, sales representatives, and agents. The more limited the lines, the more aggressive a selling effort the manufacturer can expect from that channel.

At retail there is a dazzling array of store types—department stores (Macy's), mass merchandisers (Sears and Montgomery Ward), discounters (Marshall's), specialty stores, supermarkets, mail-order houses, catalog showrooms, and box stores, as well as "neighborhoods" of stores called shopping centers. Professor Malcolm McNair, some years ago, wrote a much-discussed piece on the "wheel of retailing" in which he argued that existing retail types create their own weaknesses and thus pave the way for improved generations.[4] By his reasoning, the specialty store spawned the department store, which spawned the discounter, which spawned the cost-plus operator, and so forth. Although McNair overstates the evolutionary cycle, it is nonetheless true, as we have noted, that the channels are in constant flux and improved new variations appear to emerge endlessly.

[3] James D. Hlavacek and Tommy J. McCuistion, "Industrial Distributors—When, Who and How," *Harvard Business Review*, March–April 1983, pp. 96–101.

[4] Malcolm P. McNair, "Significant Trends and Developments in the Postwar Period," in *Competitive Distribution in a Free, High-Level Economy and Its Implications for the University*, ed. A. B. Smith (Pittsburgh: University of Pittsburgh Press, 1958), pp. 1– 25. Also see the critical discussion by Stanley C. Hollander, "The Wheel of Retailing," *Journal of Marketing*, July 1960, pp. 37–42.

Earlier we made brief reference to a fundamental question concerning the primary nature of the middleman's function: Does the middleman buy for the consumer or sell for the manufacturer? In many cases, the answer will vary depending upon one's choice of middleman, distributor or retailer. Nonetheless, the repercussions of this question are far-reaching. Historically it is reasonably evident that the middleman served the supplier. Distributors were recognized for the brands and lines they carried. But in the last decade or so there has been a noticeable shift from seller to consumer orientation. The middleman buys for the consumer. Such a switch, when one thinks about it, makes considerable sense from a marketing point of view. In fact, the better retailers today are already "thinking like manufacturers" in the sense that they are concerned about "positioning," product portfolios, segmentation, differential advantage, and strategic planning. They are buying and operating with full regard for their end-user clientele. If one pushes this logic to its extreme, the suppliers will eventually be viewed as the manufacturing arm of the channels. We'll have more to say about this when we write about the "value theory" in the next chapter.

There is a second question, somewhat related to the first, that the marketing manager of the emerging company must ponder: "Are my interests, as the manufacturer, compatible with the interests of my channels?" At first blush the answer seems to be, "Of course, we depend on each other." But some additional contemplation suggests that we had better watch out for any easy generalization. If the channels do indeed "buy" for the consumer, then the requirements of any particular supplier are secondary to the marketing programs of the distributor or retailer. The optimal strategy for seller and channel may well be at odds. Consider the likely preferences, at the extreme, of each party, as seen in the table on page 70.

What does this amount to? Channel cooperation is acquired by the seller through hard work, constant attention, aggressive marketing programs, and sensitivity to channel needs. To a large extent, the outcome goes to the aggressive: it is a power game.

Channels, we conclude, are not always what they seem. In a thoughtful article, Michael Pearson discussed what he called "distribution myths," which can be summarized as follows:[5]

---

[5] Adapted from Michael Pearson, "Ten Distribution Myths," *Business Horizons*, May–June 1981, pp. 17–23.

MARKETING ATTRIBUTE	SUPPLIER WANTS CHANNEL TO:	CHANNEL WOULD PREFER TO:
Product line	Carry full line on an exclusive basis Maintain abundant inventory	Carry best movers Carry competitive items Receive prompt shipment from supplier
Price	Shave margins Be competitive Pay promptly	Earn full margin Avoid competition with price cutters Receive extended credit terms
Organization	Provide a product manager Dedicate the sales force	Integrate product into regular organization
Advertising	Spend on advertising Aggressively market	Have supplier advertise Market the business, not the line

1. *Myth:* A channel is the movement of goals from manufacturer to consumer. *Fact:* A channel represents primarily a number of value-added attributes which facilitate the flow, such as breaking bulk, financing, and simple assembly.

2. *Myth:* A channel is determined by the nature of the products. *Fact:* The motivations of the buyer are more important.

3. *Myth:* Manufacturers manage their channels. *Fact:* This is only occasionally true.

4. *Myth:* Cooperation is the key. *Fact:* It is more important to emphasize competition so as to keep pressure on costs.

5. *Myth:* Warehouses are for storage. *Fact:* Movement of merchandise is far more important.

6. *Myth:* Manufacturers sell to wholesalers. *Fact:* This ignores the real need to sell through the wholesaler.

7. *Myth:* Costs can be reduced by eliminating the distributor. *Fact:* You can't eliminate his essential functions.

8. *Myth:* Administered channels are more efficient. *Fact:* There is no evidence that competition is less efficient.

9. *Myth:* Efficiency means profits. *Fact:* Not if competition is severe, others are better at innovating, or efficiency is incorrectly measured (it should relate to customer satisfaction).

10. *Myth:* The distribution strategy should be planned by the distribution manager. *Fact:* The decisions are so basic that top management must be involved.

COMMUNICATION STRATEGY

Later chapters (7, 8, and 9) elaborate upon the communication aspects of the marketing strategy. We shall include now only a few elementary remarks in order to balance the material dealing with the five elements of marketing strategy—product, segment, price, channels, and communications.

Communication centers on the issue of how buyers find out about the product. Communication, in this context, creates the interface between buyer and seller and is summed up usually in the expression "customer relationships."

There are four commonly recognized communication techniques: advertising, promotion and merchandising, personal selling, and public relations. These, in turn, are made up of many alternative tactical specifics: demonstrations, direct mail, displays, sales aids, incentive tools, coupons, publicity, in-house communications, seminars, and demonstration centers. The words "communication mix" say it all.

The purpose of each major communication type is reasonably apparent:

Advertising: To create consumer brand awareness and preference

Merchandising and promotion: To provide a reason for buying at the point of sale

Personal selling: To convert intention into buying action

Public relations: To inform a broad assortment of company audiences, by means other than "paid-for" media

As with so many of our business concepts, these definitions are not absolute. Some presumed consumer advertising is meant to impress retail buyers. Some personal selling is intended to create awareness or build consumer confidence. Some merchandising, as in the case of Bloomingdale's store ambience and merchandise presentation, is expected to reinforce the firm's long-term image and positioning objectives.

The marketing manager in the emerging company has the challenge of trying to combine the variables into an effective communication whole. His or her immediate objective may be to increase the productivity of the sales force, to extend the level of customer awareness, to increase trial, to gain distribution, or to open up a new segment. But because the choices are so numerous and the ramifications of the choice so great, the manager in the new enterprise has no alternative but to treat the communication strategy as a critical investment. Hence, the purpose of the communication program should be precise and clearly understood by the rest of management. It also follows that the communication effort should be consistent with the other elements of the marketing strategy.

Communication has, in the final analysis, three tasks to perform: (1) inform, (2) persuade, and (3) reinforce. Each of the three requires separate market treatment.

The information requirement boils down to the need to define the particular segment being addressed, the benefits and values sought by that segment, and the appropriate media and message by which to reach it. Experienced communicators remind us that effective messages are simple, pertinent, and repetitive.

Persuasion is a more difficult matter. It requires that we progress the prospect from informed observer to committed participant. The potential buyer usually has a number of choices as well as a set of personal priorities, which we must realign. The first sale is always the hardest—in fact, the president of The North Face affirms, "You never make money on the first purchase. It is the repeat business that counts." The significance of this point of view for the developing company is far-reaching. The marketing philosophy should be amended to imply, "To be profitable you must enlarge the base of repeat customers."

The importance of reinforcement, to turn to our third communication function, is reasonably evident. We all tend to rationalize our difficult decisions ("Wasn't I smart to buy that dress/to purchase that car/to select that college?"). After a purchase, we seek reinforcement that confirms the wisdom of our initial decision. Who do you think reads the automobile advertisement, the person who is about to buy a new car or the person who has just bought one? You can easily hear yourself as you flip through the pages of the magazine, saying, "Look at that great economy car I bought—no power brakes, no whitewalls, no power steering, four cylinders, no fancy trim. Only a sophisticated, twentieth-century genius like me would have the character to buy such a sensible car instead of getting sucked into that gross-looking Mercedes!"

The principle of reinforcement reminds us that we all rationalize our tough choices and thus become prime candidates for a repeat purchase as well as enthusiastic recommenders to our friends. Advertising, in these instances, plays its role as a postsale reinforcement. Word of mouth may well be the prime communication medium.

CLASSIFYING STRATEGIES

So much for the individual elements of strategy; let's talk now about the assembled whole. What kinds of overall strategies are there? How do successful marketing departments gain an edge in the market, this being the ultimate test of all strategies?

Corporate strategies can reflect, at the primal level, one of three business philosophies: lowest costs, most creative R&D, or the exploitation of a market niche. Texas Instruments is often singled out as the competitor that best exemplifies cost efficiency and minimum prices (which are used to buy market share), Hewlett Packard as the firm that stakes its differentiation on product innovation, and any number of specialists (Omark Industries, Saga, Crown Cork, Dr. Pepper) as those which focus on market niches.

For the emerging enterprise it would appear most prudent to play the game of "nichemanship," preferably coupled with some form of innovation. In graphic form the new enterprise can enter a market by selecting from four alternatives (see Figure 5.2). The X box is clearly a catastrophic alternative ("I'm going to challenge IBM head on!"). The ? box has its own limitations. Even in a niche the imitator can't expect to last too long, probably until the giants decide to move in.

FIGURE 5.2

	Copy	Innovation
Head on	X	✓
Niche	?	✓

Assuming that the emerging enterprise elects to focus on new products or special corners of the market (a cost approach is essentially a price-commodity game), there nonetheless is the need to develop a unique strategy, for which there are many models.

Lee Adler, in *Plotting Your Marketing Strategy*, presents a series of essays that describe separately effective approaches, including:[6]

1. *The end run,* in which the practitioner skirts around the status quo by significant innovation. Creativity is the necessary input.

2. *Concentration,* or the application of one's strength against a competitive weakness. Often such concentration is applied to segments, channels, or communication. Concentration is the rifle, as opposed to the shotgun.

3. *Market segmentation,* or the matching of product and strategy to a segment. The opposite, of course, is "one product for all," e.g., the black Ford.

4. *Market stretching,* a term we will pick up later, which embraces the concept of new uses, increased usage, and more frequent obsolescence, for expanding markets.

5. *Multibrand entries,* a favorite technique of Procter and Gamble in the detergent business. The new brand can be used for a new segment, an improved product, a different use, a change in consumer life-styles, or as a defensive ploy.

6. *Brand extension,* or using the same name for an expanded line of products—perhaps complementary (as in Black and Decker), but perhaps unrelated (as in AMF or NL Industries).

7. *Product innovation,* to many the best of all worlds, in which technology provides the cutting edge. The risk, unfortunately, is that the costs are high and the innovation may be unrelated to market needs.

8. *International expansion,* which is simply a form of segmentation.

9. *Distribution breakthroughs,* as in the case of the first department stores, supermarkets, self-service chains, discounters, fast-food operators, or shopping centers.

For those who relish lists, there is one more appended below—it is the result of a student project in which the assignment was to dream

---

[6] Lee Adler, *Plotting Marketing Strategy*, ed. Lee Adler (New York: Simon & Schuster, 1967).

up strategic opposites (the last one was obviously submitted by a biased football fan):

End Run versus Straight Onslaught
Me-Too versus Innovation
Concentration versus Shotgun
Market Segmentation versus One Product for All
Domestic versus International
Multibrand Entries versus Single Brand
Market Stretching versus Product Stretching
Brand Extension versus Specialization
Testimonials (Third Party) versus Direct Education
Reactive versus Proactive
Distractive versus Orthodox
Vertical Integration versus Horizontal
System versus Component
Internal Development versus Acquisition
Sequential versus Concurrent
Push versus Pull
The Big Bomb versus Three Yards and Cloud of Dust

Strategies are sometimes depicted in terms of matrices. The two below (Figures 5.3 and 5.4), based on the work of the Boston Consulting Group and Walker Lewis of Strategic Planning Associates, were included in a *Fortune* article:[7]

FIGURE 5.3

Number of Ways Advantage Can Be Obtained

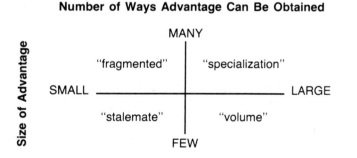

[7] Walter Kiechel III, "Three (or Four or More) Ways to Win," *Fortune*, October 19, 1981.

FIGURE 5.4

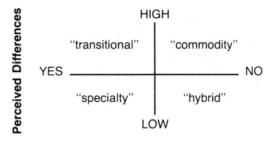

The four quadrants in Figure 5.3 require different strategies. In fragmented businesses, such as restaurants, the best strategy is minimum investment, emphasis upon efficiency, and cautious expansion. The specialization quadrant, on the other hand, calls for "managing for position" (Japanese autos). The volume competitor needs to use experience curve logic, whereas the stalemate participant (steel, paper) requires tight control and should liquidate, if possible.

The matrix in Figure 5.4 uses price and perceived differences as the differentiating dimensions.

The natural strategies are posited as shown in Figure 5.5.

FIGURE 5.5

Be prepared for competitive improvements (IBM)	Experience curve approach, market share wars (gas and steel)
Keep adding the specialty value (wines)	Avoid price wars, talk quality but don't spend much for it (salt)

SUMMARY

Marketing strategy provides the competitor with a differential advantage in the marketplace. The advantage is usually based upon two characteristics, uniqueness and execution. They can apply to any of the five elements of marketing strategy: product policy, segmentation, pricing, distribution systems, and communication.

Strategy variations are numerous—the mix, in practice, is extremely rich. There are, despite the variety, certain commonalities that characterize effective strategies, including concentration, innovation, buyer orientation, surprise, and flexibility. Good strategies are not static.

6

The Dynamics of Marketing Strategy

The more prevailing issues of marketing strategy extend beyond the taxonomy. Given that we can define the separate strategic elements and classify an assortment of strategic types, what are the influences that cause strategy to change and how does it change over time? In other words, we shall now shift our attention to the dynamics of strategy. We are concerned more with understanding than with recognition.

We are all aware, as business people, that the competitive world is a severe taskmaster: it places constant and heavy demands upon the participants. Current strategies are already somewhat obsolete. The marketing manager in the emerging company had best begin to develop immediately his or her skills at anticipating the requirements of the market. Any blind introspection or flatulence ("We have the finest reputation," "Our product is superior," "Our brand is recognized worldwide") runs the risk of costing dearly. Think of all those fine companies that were blindsided by unanticipated competitive threats—the makers of slide rules and mechanical calculators, the steel industry, Harley Davidson, the Swiss watchmakers, and the producers of vacuum tubes.

The competitive nature of any market is complex. Professor Michael Porter has eloquently described the complications and concludes that there are five competitive influences that determine the desirability of markets: 1) present competitors, 2) probability of new competitors,

3) likelihood of new technology, 4) pressure from buyers, 5) pressure from suppliers.[1]

When one contemplates the potential impact of these five influences, the need of the emerging enterprise to consider carefully the milieu it intends to enter is reinforced. Some market situations are favorable; some are not. And it is not just the current apparent situation that needs assessment. A thoughtful analysis should lead management to consider several factors: Can we make money? Are there segments or product variations we should avoid? Can we mitigate, by imaginative behavior, some of the threats? Which competitors do we prefer? Is the market worth pursuing?

Porter's analysis traces very clearly the extent to which strategy is conditioned by the competitive scene. Marketers have long advised, correctly, "Watch the customers." Porter amends that to include "and the other competitive factors."

GROWTH OPTIONS

The marketing manager, over time, has two alternative growth directions: markets and products. Each of these, in turn, has two dimensions: "present" and "new." Igor Ansoff has coupled the four into a simple diagram, Figure 6.1 (the numbering system is for identification purposes only).[2]

Box 1 implies that we plan to increase sales by selling more of our present line to more of our present markets. Not surprisingly, we label this strategic option "market penetration."

Box 2, on the other hand, suggests that we open up new markets or segments. The label? "Market development."

Box 3 is "product development" because we expand by funneling new products to our existing markets.

Box 4, the riskiest of all because it deals with unknowns in both directions, is popularly labeled "diversification" (the pessimist would call it "potential suicide").

---

[1] Adapted with permission of The Free Press, a division of Macmillan, Inc. from *Competitive Strategy: Techniques for Analyzing Industries and Competitors* by Michael E. Porter. Copyright © 1980 by The Free Press.

[2] H. Igor Ansoff, "Strategies for Diversification," *Harvard Business Review*, September–October 1957, pp. 113–124.

FIGURE 6.1

Markets

		Present	New
Products	Present	1	2
	New	3	4

In the start-up company the choices will ordinarily be constrained by time and resource limitations. Additional new-product introductions, for instance, are for the future, as is diversification (though it wouldn't hurt the manager to think early about these options). The normal management attention will be upon penetration (box 1) or market development (box 2). Is one of these two to be preferred?

The "market share" game is, needless to say, direct confrontation. If you win, the competitor loses. Sometimes it is the best game in town. There are three conditions under which it probably makes sense to favor this attack:

1. The market is growing. That hopefully means two things: your competition may not know that you are gaining relative share because their absolute volume continues to rise; the overall growth in total demand will boost the return on your market share investment.

2. You have a strategic differentiation that provides an edge in the marketplace—perhaps the product, perhaps other meaningful consumer values.

3. The major competition has shifted its emphasis to some other portion of its business, or has grown inefficient.

It is well to keep in mind that having market share may result in higher profits, but gaining market share is an expensive proposition.

There was considerable support in business during the 1970s for a fourth argument: because costs often decline predictably when cumulative experience goes up (the so-called experience curve), the smart competitor should slash prices today in order to "buy" extra volume, which results in lower costs and lower prices, et cetera, et cetera. The emerging company would be poorly advised to contemplate such a strategy—the front end costs are huge. Moreover, the strategy assumes that the only meaningful buying criterion is price. Except in the case of commodities, there is too much evidence to the contrary. Buyers prefer a wider range of values. That's the logic of market segmentation!

The second likely growth option for the emerging enterprise is "present products in new markets." It makes sense to launch your product(s) in several segments; not only do you spread your risks, but you preempt your competition. Because resources are limited, the marketing manager will no doubt be tempted to "go for volume" and sell whatever he can and wherever he can. That's a mistake! It just dissipates the proprietary strengths of the new firm. Concentration is as important in business strategy as it is in military. Nichemanship is almost always the surest course for the embryonic competitor.

The matrix approach to the four growth options can be made considerably more useful, particularly for the emerging enterprise, if we "stretch" the two dimensions, markets and products.

Consider first the market axis. We can sell more to our present markets, without taking (absolute) volume from our competitors, if we are able to develop among buyers new uses, greater usage, or faster replacement. If successful, we have "stretched" our market horizon. Likewise, we can multiply the product options by listing ways to enhance the product offer, including repositioning, advertising, packaging, delivery system innovations, special pricing, and so on. Our little two-by-two matrix now becomes a useful tool for considering growth alternatives and strategies (see Figure 6.2). This diagram, because of the two-way stretch, helps us realistically to develop specific operational strategies. For example, if "new uses" is our "market" stretching selection, what product mix should we assemble to best realize this selection? The market columns, to be even more functional, can be subdivided into separate segments and product strategies assembled for each.

Is it better for the emerging enterprise to concentrate on market stretching or product stretching? On the assumption that the new firm

FIGURE 6.2

Markets

	Present	New Uses	More Usage	Faster Replacement	New
Systems Image Delivery Packaging Brand Promotion Positioning etc. etc. New					

has a unique offer, there is no point in manipulating the offer variables (except perhaps for particular segments). Why not, instead, emphasize the market stretching options?

The commodity firm, by comparison, has the reverse problem. It badly needs a unique offer—a stretching of the product dimension.

GROWTH MARKETS OR MATURE MARKETS?

One of the risks of living in Santa Clara County ("Silicon Valley"), California, is the contagious assumption that all businesses are high tech, volatile, and fast-growing. Growth becomes the fetish; one forgets that most business operates in a more traditional setting. We have to remind ourselves that mature industries also represent first-class opportunities for the new enterprise. There are many envied companies that thrive in "ordinary" markets. Despite a more static primary demand, they outperform their competitors.

Growth industries, to be sure, have many attractions. The environment is exciting, the internal pace quickens, there are plenty of career opportunities, everyone can hope to ride the bandwagon, and the investment community looks with favor upon those competitors that accept new opportunities. But there are dangers:

- There is need by the competitor for a large front-end investment, as well as a series of ongoing investments that at least match the industry's growth rate.

- Technology explodes, and creates as many uncertainties as it does opportunities.
- Competition is fierce, typically from fast-moving start-ups.
- Short time cycles make it all too easy for the firm to develop internal weaknesses that are concealed by the fast growth (growth often "hides the warts").
- The new markets and products are somewhat beyond the traditional areas of company expertise.
- The possibility of loss is high.

The risk of new ventures was vividly highlighted in a recent study by Ralph Biggadike.[3] From a sample of eighty-six companies he reports:

1. The typical corporate venture suffers harsh losses through its first four years.
2. New ventures take eight years, on the average, to become profitable.
3. It takes ten to twelve years before the ROI of the ventures is equal to that of the mature businesses.
4. The average new venture is able to acquire only 10% market share after four years.
5. The biggest losers, in terms of ROI, are firms with the smallest entry scale.
6. Most managers set too low initial market share targets, namely 10%.

Perhaps the greatest danger of our all-out drive for growth opportunities is that management takes its eye off its mature product/market business. It is not uncommon to hear management conclude, "We'll manage our existing businesses for cash, and invest the extra money into growth situations." More often than not, such a philosophy is devastating to the mature businesses. For example, R&D slows down, emphasis shifts to process improvements, the best people migrate out of the operation (who wants to be identified with a cash cow or, worse still, a dog?), a commodity mentality takes over, and the operation becomes ripe for plucking.

During the last ten years this is exactly what happened to some of

---

[3] Ralph Biggadike, "The Risky Business of Diversification," *Harvard Business Review*, May–June 1979, pp. 103–111.

our established industries. The Japanese, as a case in point, ignored the "manage for cash" advice and captured large portions of steelmaking, automobiles, cameras, motorcycles, home entertainment, banking, appliances, calculators, watches, and office machines, to name but a few. And these businesses were mostly so-called mature industries. The Japanese elected to invest heavily, and through quality, innovation, a strong customer orientation, efficient production, and heavy marketing efforts they managed to turn the tables on the traditional suppliers. While the traditionalists managed "mature markets," the Japanese decided that *maturity and growth are man-made definitions and a market is largely what you can make of it.* Although there are certainly some mature businesses that have reached the end of their lives, there are many more whose stagnation is a function of how the participants do business. Innovation, in these situations, can open up unexpected growth potentials. How about breakthroughs in marketing (BMW's nichemanship, Black and Decker's line extension, McDonald's fast-food approach), technology (transistors instead of vacuum tubes, jet engines instead of piston, hand-held calculators instead of desk-top), design (Casio, Canon, and Seiko), quality (Japanese cars), operations ("just-in-time inventory" and quality circles) and merchandising (L'eggs)?

Perhaps we can best wrap it up by saying that if you find yourself in an untenable market position, consider several possible courses of action:

- Innovate (if you have the creativity).
- Buy market share (if you have the funds).
- Concentrate your resources.
- Change the technology.
- Find a niche.
- Reposition.
- Pray, and hope that the key competitors are tolerant.
- Withdraw by liquidation.

Above all else, remember there is the distinct possibility that there are no mature markets, only mature managers!

THE PRODUCT LIFE CYCLE

We briefly referred earlier to the specialty commodity continuum as "the product life cycle" and described how competitors position and reposition themselves along the line. What interests us at this point is how, and why, marketing strategy changes over the cycle. This inquiry is of utmost importance to the emerging enterprise because management must anticipate the changes that are likely to occur, and redirect the strategy.

The product life cycle (PLC) is generally drawn as an S curve and subdivided into several stages (see Figure 6.3).

You undoubtedly have already recognized that the slope of the curve and the distances between stages are arbitrary. Indeed, if we could accurately draw these curves before the fact, marketing strategy would be a snap. Notwithstanding, we aren't completely naive about the nature of these cycles.

First, we are cautious about them. We appreciate, for example, that they are probably more useful conceptually than they are operationally. How many business managers, would you guess, allow their products to run through the cycle to eventual decline? Not many. Rather they alter, modify, and reformulate the products so as to restimulate the curve (see Figure 6.4).

It is thus not easy to recognize when an original product has been modified into a new one with its own cycle. Furthermore, an existing curve implies certain volume/time relationships that could be substantially altered by the innovative approach of a new competitor— GOR-TEX in fabrics, Sinclair in consumer electronics, or Savin in

FIGURE 6.3

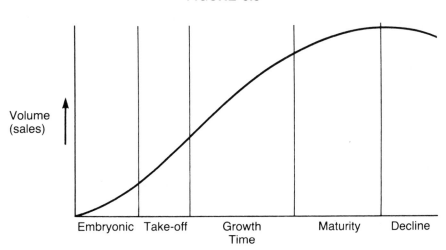

FIGURE 6.4

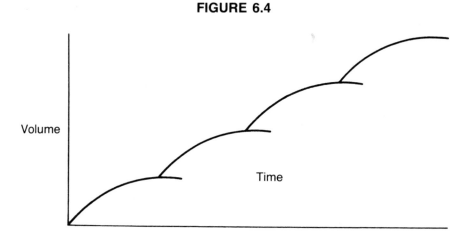

copiers. The curves, in other words, shift. They might stretch, they might shrink. Nonetheless, the PLC is useful. How?

First, many marketers have recognized through experience that the appropriate marketing strategy is related to "stage in the life cycle." Theodore Levitt addresses this question in his article, "Exploit the Product Life Cycle."[4] He suggests how advertising, pricing, selling, and so on, should vary in form and importance over time.

A second approach has been to couple the PLC with market share and generalize strategies in those two dimensions, as the table on the next page illustrates.

The trouble with these descriptions is just that: they describe more than they explain why. But for the emerging company the *why* is essential because the initial strategy ordinarily will decide the future of the operation.

WHY, OR THE VALUE THEORY

The theory: As a product matures and moves through its life cycle, the product-related values that the user is willing to pay for shift into the channels (or the sales force), and this shift dictates important strategic alterations.

The explanation: Assume that your company has just invented a

---

[4] Theodore Levitt, "Exploit the Product Life Cycle," *Harvard Business Review*, November–December 1965, pp. 81–94.

Stages of the Product Life Cycle

	GROWTH	MATURITY	DECLINE
Domination	Invest in operations Reduce prices Utilize capacity fully Heavy R & D investment	Full line Aggressive sales and advertising Cost reduction Aggressive distribu- tion policy	Liquidate some mar- ket share Trim the line Adopt commodity approach
Also-ran	Invest to build share Segment where you can dominate Specialize	Cost focus Stress productivity Imitate	Withdraw

new packaged consumer goods specialty, "a healthful carbonated protein drink" called Vigor. The product is clearly in the stage of *innovation* in the product life cycle. (We shall alter, for our purposes, the traditional PLC stages and titles.) Your firm is the only supplier of this item— there are no imitators (yet). Neither the trade nor the consumers have a choice in regard to your brand; they deal with you or no one.

As marketing manager of this emerging enterprise, your most urgent need is to create awareness. So your earliest expenditures will be for advertising, particularly since you are operating in a consumer market. In theory, you would spend almost all of your marketing dollars on awareness so as to build a brand franchise and consumer pull as quickly as possible. But some wholesalers and retailers, for reasons of their own, will drag their feet in stocking the product. Their reticence may not be rational (if the product really represents a significant consumer value), but it is typical nonetheless. In order not to waste your advertising dollars by having spotty distribution, you will "buy" the trade's cooperation with deals and promotions (special dollar inducements). How much? Probably in some such proportion as 75 percent advertising and 25 percent promotion. This split reflects your innovative pull modified by some degree of channel leverage (if they don't stock, we don't sell). Generally, however, in this innovative period the marketing strength lies with the innovator who can concentrate on creating consumer interest.

But the innovative stage doesn't last long—sometimes seventeen years (as in the case of patents) and sometimes a day or so (try the clothing design business!). Let's assume that your protein drink runs away with the market for a year or two. Then, inevitably, some competitors spring up, each with its own perfectly good, healthful protein drink alternative. Your brand may have the highest consumer recognition, but nonetheless the consumer and the trade (the customer) now have the choice. They don't have to buy your brand. Generally, in packaged consumer goods, brand preference is much higher than brand loyalty. I may prefer X but I'll take Y under such conditions as out of stock, lower price, special promotion, or a friend's suggestion.

At this moment in time we shall label your stage in the PLC as *imitation*. Whereas the consumer, during innovation, had to patronize the particular stores that carried your brand, now the consumer can shop anywhere knowing there will be an acceptable substitute. So the buyer chooses a store for a number of shopping reasons such as location, ambience, fresh vegetable reputation, meat department, or credit terms. The retailers' values are greater than the manufacturers'!

The manufacturer is now in a secondary position and has no real choice but to pay the retailer for his support: that is, deals and promotions will jump to perhaps 60 percent, while advertising drops to 40 percent. (The shift, not the absolute numbers, is the important point.)

The third stage—*price reduction*—is born when deals and promotions by the soft drink competitors have become so intense (every week some brand is "on deal") that the consumer forgets the normal price reference point. "Drinks are not fifty cents a can—they're twenty cents!" On this inevitable day the manufacturers have to reduce permanently their prices to the new consumer expectation. A dark day indeed!

Now the industry has gone full cycle. To escape the commodity trap the manufacturer must innovate with a new product and start the game all over:

	1. Innovation	{ Advertising 75% { Deals 25%
New product	2. Imitation	{ Deals 60% { Advertising 40%
	3. Permanent price cut	{ No deals { No advertising

There are several important changes in strategy dictated by this cycle. First, the manufacturer moves from a pull approach (stage 1) to a push approach (stage 2). Second, the retailer becomes an equal, if not more powerful, marketing player. Third, the sales force replaces the advertising (brand) manager as the dominant marketing influence in the supplier's firm. Fourth, the nature of the advertising shifts from product values to images and perceptions.

To the extent that this theory is reasonable, the observer would expect that in stage 2 the store labels (private/house brands) would inevitably replace the national labels, which in turn would become price brands. But, in reality, this erosion has seldom occurred, at least in the packaged consumer goods field. Private labels, including generics, have held at about 40 percent of overall sales for the past two decades (though this percentage does vary by category), and the national labels have maintained their prices. How has this occurred?

In the first place, the major manufacturers are strong marketers and are positioned as "marketing experts." The expertise of such marketing giants as Procter and Gamble, General Foods, and Pillsbury is recognized by the trade. This means that the retailers will support a number of "standard" new-too products under the umbrella of those manufacturers' general marketing programs.

Second, the manufacturers have "bent the arrow" successfully. Their advertising and merchandising efforts have created brand images and perceptions that pay off in meaningful buying preferences, if not absolute loyalty.

Third, the major producers have worked hard at developing high-quality products that establish a preference base of consumer acceptance for national labels.

Does this value theory apply to the industrial markets as well, particularly where much of the distribution is by direct selling? It most certainly does, and that becomes evident if some of the consumer goods vocabulary is transformed:

STAGE OF PLC	CONSUMER GOODS	INDUSTRIAL GOODS
Innovation	Advertising, brand manager, distributor	Scientist/engineer, product manager, selling
Imitation	Deals and promotions Retail/wholesale	Salespeople, service, back-up support
Price reduction	Commodity	Commodity

For the emerging enterprise the lessons are meaningful. Over time, be prepared for a shift from product values to sales force or distribution values. That requires a hefty change in the marketing mix and a powerful impetus toward commodity selling. Salvation will depend upon your ability to "turn the arrow" back. The incompetent marketing manager is the one who leads the firm directly from innovation to price reduction.

THE SPECIAL CASE OF HIGH TECHNOLOGY

Of particular interest to many emerging enterprises is the special case of high technology. Not only does this case have all the pros and cons of a growth business, but additional special circumstances that complicate the marketing job (though, as we shall see, most of the basic marketing concepts are still applicable).

What, we must first ask, is "high technology"? Every manager, when asked, seems to be in it, but only a few meet the requirements of the definition: *High technology includes those industries—bio-medical, micro-processors, optics, telecommunications, lasers—where operations are profoundly and continuously impacted by breakthroughs in product technology.*[5]

As a result we would classify a chemical company, a refinery, or a jet engine builder as complex technology but not high. Rapid profound change is the key. Rapid profound change vastly complicates the life of any manager, particularly in an emerging company. Consider these six consequences (which, of course, have major marketing consequences):

1. Ongoing product and technology advances. This means that the entire company, not just marketing or production, must be able to respond appropriately. As a matter of fact, these firms are constantly adapting. The size of the market, as well as its direction, is difficult to estimate. Costs are virtually impossible to pin down early in the development cycle. Investment decisions are tough to make, and it is preferable that new equipment be flexible, versatile, and compatible with the existing equipment. The need to adapt highlights the need for better-than-average market antennae. *Customer awareness is as important as technology.*

2. Short life cycles. Time is of the essence, owing to the fast-changing scene. This means that the company's business strategies and tactics

---

[5] Some of the comments that follow were adapted from an in-house document prepared by Management Analysis Center, Cambridge, Massachusetts.

must be under steady review, such as those covering inventory policies, the marketing mix, and the service definition. The evolution from specialty to commodity can be very rapid and the time for innovation minimal. Under these conditions it is difficult to get back R&D investments. There is also a difficult production issue: "Do we build capacity in advance, when the limits of the technology are not yet evident?" The normal condition in high-tech industries is that capacity is limited.

3. Creativity versus the orderly analytic life. High-tech firms are long on creativity and short on analytic/administrative skills. The entrepreneur is an individual with new ideas and approaches who thrives on the untried. As his or her firm grows, there is a tug of war between the analytic and the creative. The traditional outside financial world prefers order and precision and so leaves these burgeoning entrepreneurs to a special subset of financial investors called venture capitalists. With growth there continues to be a struggle to keep the two philosophies in some kind of balance—to keep the administrative from destroying the creative.

4. A difficult sale. The high-tech salesperson has two responsibilities: to sell the new technology and to sell its application. This duality requires that the seller work closely with the customer, particularly during the product design stages, and provide technical support and considerable hand-holding. Because the customer requires as much planning time as possible where new technologies are involved, he must be "in" early on the new technology. Furthermore, the customer needs assurance that the price/performance ratio for the new technology will work to his or her advantage (as has occurred in semiconductors and computers).

Finally, because the shift from technology to low-cost application is usually rapid, the seller must be prepared to move with the buyer in a telescoped time frame. This implies that *precise customer targeting is necessary.*

5. Complex organizational needs. High-tech organizations have unusual problems. For example, it is unreasonable in these companies to confine each business function to an exact organizational box. Whereas R&D, engineering, manufacturing, and marketing in a consumer goods company are easily separated, this is much less true in a high-technology firm. Where R&D ends and engineering begins is not always clear; engineering may produce the first dozen pieces before transferring the plans and dies to manufacturing; R&D may make the first sales (to scientists). People must learn to play different roles and behave in a less structured way.

The use of task forces is a natural, given these conditions. Each team is formed around a particular project that has its own functional priorities. In one military airframe company, for example, there were twenty-three task forces one year, one for each of twenty-three key sales targets. Each task force had representatives from the different functions, and a chairman. But the chairman could come from any one of the functions (e.g., R&D, engineering, costing, sales), depending on which was most sensitive at that time in the contract's evolution.

6. New markets. Finally, the constant emergence of new markets in high-tech firms requires that the marketing manager be open-minded about new and novel marketing approaches. He or she must be able to offer new segments an appropriate choice of product, information, distribution channels, selling approaches, price alternatives, and service.

CUSTOMER CREATION

All of these strategic notions—whether they be growth or mature industries, consumer goods or industrial, low tech or high tech—rotate around the need to create customers. As we said earlier, that's what marketing is all about. As a consequence, it will help the manager of the emerging company to understand some of the customer creation structure that others have used successfully. We shall refer to three: The adoption cycle, the diffusion process, and Montgomery's buying model.

The Adoption Cycle

The adoption cycle hypothesizes how an individual customer comes into being: it describes the progressive steps necessary to convert a prospective buyer into a real one. Because each step must have its own mix of marketing variables, the theory is a guide to assembling a marketing strategy over time.

There are five steps in the adoption cycle:

> Awareness   Trial
> Interest   Repeat
> Conviction

Unless you and I, as prospective purchasers, know about the new service, there is no way we can consider making a purchase. Awareness can be created in several ways, as by advertising, word of mouth, display, direct mail, or personal solicitation. Awareness alone, however, will not guarantee a purchase; the prospect must have his interest aroused ("I think that's a good idea!"). Interest surely depends upon the relevance of the idea and the suitability of the communication. But interest, by itself, is also a necessary but not sufficient step. The prospective buyer needs to internalize his or her interest ("I think for me that's a good idea!"). Now we're getting closer, and the reader is probably already visualizing a number of marketing variables that would enhance this critical stage of conviction. Following conviction presumably comes trial and then, if the prospect's expectations are satisfied, repeat purchase.

The adoption cycle reminds the manager of an important marketing truism, each stage requires its own tailor-made application. A marketing strategy is not a miscellaneous collection of ways to spend money. Rather, it is a particular assemblage of marketing variables intended to move the buyer along the cycle. Advertising, for example, may play a key role in establishing awareness, but a small role in encouraging trial.

There are some additional comments about the adoption cycle that are worth mention. The five steps are not absolute. Some managers like to insert *comprehension* between "conviction" and "trial," or *repeat in depth* after "repeat" (to include the heavy buyer). Most advertising specialists prefer *aided recall* and *unaided recall* to "awareness." Nor is it necessary that the steps occur sequentially, though they usually do. How many times, for example, have you been contacted by a demonstrator in a grocery store who proffers a special nibble of cheese with the words, "Would you like to try . . ." In this case, trial comes first. Or you may have buying situations where there is no trial in the conventional sense, or less repeat. How about the Spanish government buying a dam or a hydroelectric plant from Bechtel?

Notice specifically how the adoption cycle helps to identify an appropriate marketing mix. At the top of the next page, we have sketched in a hypothetical marketing outline (for our protein soft drink) to illustrate the point. Similar formats can be drawn up for any kind of product or service.

The Diffusion Process

Whereas the adoption cycle is centered on the creation of individual customers, the diffusion process views each individual as a member

AWARENESS	INTEREST AND CONVICTION	TRIAL	REPEAT
Advertising content, reach, and frequency	Testimonials	Sales promotions	Price
	Retailer programs	Coupons	Quality rein-forcement efforts
	Merchandising	Samples	
Unique product	Co-op advertising	Distribution	Word of mouth
Direct mail		Displays	
Family brand name			

of a group and then traces how and when each group enters the market. The groups are segments and, as such, can be separately described— a useful way of applying segmentation theory. The diffusion theory establishes the segments, and their relative importance, as follows:

SEGMENT	PERCENTAGE OF TOTAL
1. Innovators	2.5%
2. Early adopters	13.5
3. Early majority	34.0
4. Late majority	34.0
5. Laggards	16.0
	100.0%

It is normally argued that:

1. The segments can be separately defined.
2. They enter the market sequentially.
3. There is no guarantee that any new product will progress all the way through. Rejection can occur at any point.
4. Because the segments are homogeneous, there have to be separate strategies for each.[6]

---

[6] These comments are based on Everett Rogers, Diffusion of Innovation (New York: The Free Press, 1962).

Once again we see that a marketing strategy must be specific to the target audience and responsive to the sequential creation of customer groups from start to finish.

Diffusion theory has had a number of practical applications. Most of us are familiar, for example, with the "opinion leader" approach, wherein the strategist tries initially to attract the innovators and early adopters by appealing to them specifically. He hopes that the rest of the market will follow. Such pyramiding is common to the introduction of new drugs to doctors and instruments to the medical market as well as in the case of luxury goods (vacation condominiums) and high fashion (dress styles).

The Montgomery Buying Model

Still another approach to customer creation that the emerging enterprise should find useful is the Montgomery buyer model. David Montgomery, of the Stanford Graduate School of Business, developed the model on behalf of a major grocery chain that was concerned about how its store buyers decided to buy or not to buy new items offered by suppliers. Montgomery's replication of their decision-making process was ingenious and allowed him to predict the actual decisions with more than 90 percent accuracy.

To the buyers, a new product was either "unique" or it was "me-too." And the seller was either well known and respected or not. The decisions were: buy if the product is unique and the seller well known; don't buy if the product is me-too and the seller unknown; buy in the other two instances only if the sales presentation is effective and the promotion package attractive. The matrix is shown in Figure 6.5.

FIGURE 6.5

Product

	Unique	Me-Too
Seller — Well known	Buy	Buy if sales presentation and promotion are impressive
Not well known	Buy if sales presentation and promotion are impressive	Don't buy

Notice that the emerging company has several strategies it can pursue, some long-range and some immediate. Over the long pull, for example, the emerging enterprise might invest in advertising and/or R&D—to establish reputation and uniqueness. Or, in the short term, it might concentrate on sales presentation and promotion packages.

We would suggest that a similar model applies to industrial firms— again assuming the substitution of certain words and mix specifics. For example, try guarantees and service in place of promotions.

The Hyler Hypotheses

One of the most imaginative recent analyses of strategy that has appeared was developed by Fletcher Hyler, a Stanford MBA and at the time a marketing manager with Digital Equipment Corporation. His analysis, which is only in unpublished form, combines many of the ideas and concepts considered above, but he takes his observations to a wider-ranging conclusion. Hyler uses the world of computers as his reference. For many of the managers of emerging firms, the applicability of the Hyler hypotheses is apparent.

1. Buyers (of computers) can be ranged on a scale of "dependence upon the seller" from low to high:

Dependence

Low   High

2. These buyers mirror the diffusion curve:

Innovator   Early majority   Late majority   Laggards

3. The seller provides pertinent values to the segments:

Hardware   Software   Service   Experience

4. With time (computers become standard), all dependence disappears and the curve swings back.

Low   Dependence   High

5. Manufacturers can be viewed as:

Boutique

                                                                        Systems house

        Commodity house

a. The Boutique manufacturer is an assembler of the latest technology. Time to market is critical. His emphasis is product marketing, i.e., sell the technical aspects.
b. The Systems enterprise, on the other hand, represents expertise and experience across the line. Buyers at this stage seek reassurance, reputation, foolproof systems, confidence. The seller does "position marketing."
c. The Commodity supplier standardizes, minimizes costs, and emphasizes simplicity.

Hyler then demonstrates how all facets of corporate strategy must be consistent with the firm's position in the cycle. For example, manufacturing policies would vary considerably among Boutique, Systems, and Commodity. So, too, would marketing, engineering, and finance. Finally, the individual firm should be sure that each of its functions has the same internal positioning.

SUMMARY

Marketing strategy is dynamic. It is continuously under siege by the competitive world. For the emerging enterprise it is mandatory, therefore, that its growth strategy reflect the inherent strengths of the firm.

Growth can be established in two directions: markets and products. If these concepts are "stretched," the resulting graph is handy for developing strategic details. One word of caution: mature markets may be just as attractive as growth markets.

Marketing strategy is dependent upon the product life cycle, the value theory suggesting that values and strategies shift over the cycle. The impact of the cycle is particularly dominant in high-tech companies, where the time cycles are so short and the impact of change so continuous.

All strategy essentially deals with creating customers. Hence the importance of considering the adoption cycle, the diffusion process, the Montgomery buying model, and the impressive strategic ideas of Fletcher Hyler.

7

Communication

Communication is the link between buyer and seller:

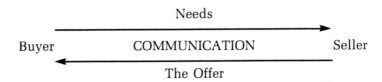

The buyer has needs; the seller makes an offer. The point of contact between the two parties is where "it all happens." A successful linkage means a sale, otherwise not. The monetary value of this interface to a going concern is, as one can guess, enormous. Just imagine the dollars involved if your company had to reestablish from ground zero its cumulative customer relationships. Not surprisingly, this communication link represents one of the major investments for the emerging company. It follows that careful planning by the marketing manager is required.

Communication, as we noted earlier, takes a number of forms. Consider the representative classification scheme seen in the table on page 99.

The possible combinations are almost countless. Nonetheless, despite this variability there are several generic approaches that are common. To provide one illustration, the manager can elect to either "push" or "pull."

To pull means to create consumer demand by direct appeal. Advertising and direct mail illustrate efforts to initiate such consumer action. On the other hand, the manager can push the product through the channels of distribution by employing salespeople or independent representatives. Selling effort, in these cases, originates in the channels, and the pressure to buy is directed at the consumer.

SELLING	ADVERTISING	PROMOTION AND MERCHANDISING	PUBLIC RELATIONS
Direct sales force	Media (radio, TV, magazines)	Consumer deals (samples, coupons, premium offers)	Corporate image
Independent representatives	Direct mail	Trade deals (display allowances, free goods, buying allowances)	Internal communication
Distributors	"Co-op" advertising		New product releases
Demonstration centers	Trade advertising		
Application laboratories	Catalogs	Sales force promotions (prizes, contests, awards)	
Retail stores		Store ambience	
Telemarketing		Product presentation	
Seminars		Choice of merchandise	

Which approach is better for the emerging enterprise? Customer awareness, as we showed earlier, is the first order of business for the seller. It would appear, therefore, that a pull strategy is to be preferred. Pull can create either a user preference or a channel decision to carry the brand. But pull is a seller expense (at least in the early days of the enterprise) and, to reach the threshold of visibility, advertising may be too expensive. Advertising is likely, moreover, to broadside the market and thus prove somewhat inefficient, unless the segmentation strategy is sound. And advertising takes time. Not surprisingly, for these reasons the initial temptation for the emerging company is to place most of its chips on salesman/channel efforts. Theirs is the hope that buying pressure will be generated by these intermediaries. Unfortunately, as we noted briefly, the expectation is generally greater than the realization. Distributors and retailers are better at selling existing lines than pioneering new ones. In the final analysis, therefore, a push strategy requires considerable support from the manufacturer.

The choice between push and pull is also dependent upon additional influences, such as the size and accessibility of the market (advertising may be too expensive in small, scattered territories), the uniqueness of the product (advertising may quickly gain consumer awareness), the degree and nature of competition (the established companies may "own" the traditional channels of distribution), and the speed of product launch (both push and pull might be needed to ensure early market domination).

Communication variables can be described further in terms of their impact upon demand (sales). So-called demand elasticity varies over the communication range. Traditionally, we have treated price as the most sensitive determinant of sales. That may often be true, but not always. Demand elasticity, we have seen, can also be a function of advertising, promotion, sales effectiveness, product image, distribution policies, packaging, or samples. What do you consider the most important factor in the sale of luxury cars? of complex medical equipment? of fast food?

Deciding the communication mix is no mean task. The characteristics of each communication variable, for example, must be recognized as well as the synergistic possibilities of certain combinations. One suggested sorting scheme indicates dramatically how the variables compare in terms of six criteria (additional criteria would, of course, yield different comparisons):

COMMUNICATION VARIABLE	MEASUREMENT CRITERIA					
	Cost per 1,000	Potential Reach	Target Selectivity	Probable Impact	Flexibility	HQ Control
Advertising	Low	High	Low	Low	Low	High
Promotions	↓	↓	↓	↓	↓	↓
Co-op ads						
Direct mail						
Catalogs						
Trade shows						
Demo centers						
Seminars						
Telemarketing						
Retail stores						
Personal selling						
Executive selling						
National account management	High	Low	High	High	High	Low

Notice, by this ranking, how the desirability of the variables changes, depending upon the measurement.

The choice of communication variables differs between consumer goods, industrial goods, and service companies. The lists that follow are a reasonable summary of these differences.

RELATIVE RANKING OF COMMUNICATION VARIABLES

Consumer Goods	Industrial Goods	Services (Intangibles)
Advertising	Personal selling	Advertising and word of mouth
Merchandising and promotion	Merchandising and promotion	Merchandising and promotion
Personal selling	Advertising	Public relations
Public relations	Public relations	Personal selling

Consumer goods and industrial goods companies are stereotyped as relying on advertising or personal selling. The intangibles rely on advertising and satisfied customers but place heavy emphasis upon merchandising and public relations—the ambience of the surroundings and the public image. Public relations is last in all four cases, but assumes a significant role.

Philip Kotler maintains that there is a further shift in relative importance *over the adoption cycle,* regardless of the type of market. The most dramatic shift is from advertising to personal selling as the markets mature and the potential consumers convert to actual buyers.[1] This observation supports well our earlier conclusions about the value theory. Selling, on the other hand, as we noted in our first table, is expensive— notice "cost per 1,000."

It may be useful to draw some thumbnail sketches of the major communication variables and highlight their key attributes:

Advertising

An open presentation ("everyone" can read or see the ads)
Impersonal
Broadside (it covers lots of people)
One-way communication
Flexible in the long run, inflexible in the short run

---

[1] Philip Kotler, *Marketing Management: Analysis, Planning and Control,* 4th ed. (Englewood Cliffs, N.J.: Prentice-Hall, 1980), p. 491.

Personal Selling

One-to-one

Adaptive (on the spot)

Persuasive (a mix of words, personality, personal relationships, body language)

Two-way interchange (it requires some kind of feedback)

Merchandising and Promotions

Immediate and compelling

Subliminal impact (particularly the merchandising)

Demeaning for the product (particularly the promotions)

More flexible for the seller than a price cut

Public Relations

Confidence creation

Unexpected

Taps new emotions about the product

There is an important real-life economic lesson to be learned by the emerging company when assembling its communication strategy. Much of the mix is made up of subjective services for which it is hard to identify clear value/price trade-offs. It's amazing how much bids by alternative suppliers of these services can vary—200, 300 percent, for example. So shop around. Concentrate on hiring a good advertising agency—not the biggest but the one that matches your needs for attention, speed, growth, and general relevance. Remember that you are making a significant investment, even though your initial budget is modest. You should figure the investment as your yearly budget times the expected life of your agency relationship.

ADVERTISING AND CORPORATE COMMUNICATION

Textbook coverage of advertising usually starts with descriptions of various publics or audiences that a company should address in its communication program. These audiences are ever-present, distinct in their interests and in the manner in which they can be reached. Such audiences range from employees, customers, and suppliers to shareholders and the business and financial communities; from local communities and the general public to acquisition candidates and potential employees at the college or university level. Obviously, these audiences overlap. Any message directed to the general public will more than likely hit other groups. But the optimal means for reaching each group is somewhat different.

Advertising plays a vital role in reaching many of them, but it is by no means the only company "message" that is received. The believability of an advertisement is a function of the company's total impression on the outside world. All organizations, in this regard, constantly transmit an assortment of marketing signals that reinforce, or contradict, any printed claims—all the way from the menu in the restaurant, to the decor of the doctor's office, to the physical surroundings of the corporate headquarters or the attitude of the personnel. Saga Corporation's magnificent headquarters reinforce the firm's quality message, as does the incredible service attitude of Nordstrom's retail clerks. In other words, it's a waste of time to trumpet that "we stand for quality in all our products" when the other observable attributes of the enterprise contradict this boast.

A corporation's initial message, then, should incorporate its basic values. What, in other words, does the company stand for? Why is it a desirable place to devote your working life? And equally important, how do the company values translate into great pride of accomplishment among the employees?

The above-mentioned firm, Saga Corporation (restaurants and contract feeding) defines its values as follows:

The Saga Way:

To provide maximum satisfaction for our customers—through quality performance, thoughtful personalized service, and efficient and effective operations.

To maintain the highest ethical relationships—with our customers, employees, suppliers, and competitors.

To earn satisfactory long-run profits—so as to maintain the health of the company and assure the availability of the necessary capital for continuing growth.

To develop and maintain a superior management team—dedicated to the objectives of the firm.

To assure our employees of fair and equitable compensation—and the opportunity for individual self-expression and continuous personal growth.

To anticipate the future needs of our customers and develop the plans necessary to meet these needs and ensure growth.

To fulfill our obligations to our free competitive society—by constantly developing new and improved techniques, methods, and procedures which will assure our progress and growth.

These annunciated values, when treated seriously, create among the employees great pride in the company's accomplishments and the realization that the firm's achievements have a purpose beyond economic gain.

How does an organization create these base values? One good way is to assemble the best people and have them debate and decide on a short list of reasonably attainable objectives. This list will serve as the boundaries for a consistent and coherent pattern of public communication.

One word of caution: don't try to be what you are not. The history of corporate communications is replete with examples that reinforce this admonishment. A dramatic example was Chase Manhattan Bank's competitive advertising campaign for new customers, which was launched with the slogan "You have a friend at Chase Manhattan." This statement might have been a great idea for a country bank, but not a behemoth in New York City with its guards, forbidding interior, and hostile tellers' windows. The campaign won awards for being imaginative, fresh, and new, but not for gaining new accounts.

EMPLOYEES AS AN AUDIENCE

Company employees are probably the critical audience. No firm will reach its goals if its people don't have faith and pride in themselves and their enterprise. They must be excited about what they are doing: they must *want* to perform well. As one president said, "Give me a turned-on organization and I can beat anyone." The single most important job of the president is to define the business and communicate why it is an exciting place to work.

As a corollary, management must convince employees that top-notch performance is expected from everyone. Look at IBM. Why is it where it is today? Its employees take themselves seriously; they know winning is everything; they find working for IBM intense but fun; and they know that the company imposes high standards upon each, and rewards for achieving those standards. IBM understands the psychology of motivating people. They single out individuals for note-worthy achievement, but blame everyone for failures. Label someone a loser, and he or she will start to act like one. On the other hand, psychologists agree that people need peak experiences and meaning in their lives to perform effectively.

Equally important, management must demonstrate to its employees that it is humane, that it listens and cares. This doesn't mean, however, a loose management style. Almost all the founders and leaders of the top profit-making companies today were tough as nails when their core values of service and quality were violated. But they also treated people as adults, provided training and development opportunities, and considered all as members of the winning team. The better companies have learned the trick of pairing a tough, winning attitude with a caring spirit.

What communication program will help fan the employees' enthusiasm? First, the company should seek ways to recognize those accomplishments important for achieving its goals. For example, recognize the salesperson with the highest sales, the scientist with the most patents or papers, and the secretary with the best output. But also ask the employees for their involvement. One consumer goods chief executive has pointed out, "We have finally discovered that our most effective goal is to be best at a limited number of things. We now try to get our people to help us work out what these things should be, how to define 'best' objectively, and how to become best in our selected spheres. You would be surprised at how motivating this has become."

Internal communication plays a big part in establishing such an environment. Management can disseminate information about the accomplishments and other group activities through a company-wide news network. When Edward Carlson was president of United Airlines, he said, "Nothing is worse for morale than lack of information down in the ranks. I call it NETMA—'nobody ever tells me anything'—and I have tried hard to minimize that complaint."

Informal communication can be just as beneficial as formal. Some of the better companies start with an insistence on informality. Disney is emphatic about first names, while Hewlett-Packard treats "MBWA" (Management By Wandering Around) as a major tenet of the all-important "HP Way." IBM devotes a lot of time and energy to open-door policies, getting management out of the office, and holding meetings.

The highly popular book *In Search of Excellence* concludes that the excellent companies really are close to their customers.[2] Other

---

[2] Thomas J. Peters and Robert H. Waterman, *In Search of Excellence* (New York: Harper & Row, 1982).

companies talk about it; the excellent companies do it. In fact, what the study found most striking was the consistent obsession of these firms with quality, reliability, and service. The outstanding companies are also better at finding a niche for themselves, which they do by listening to their customers.

How can a communications program bring the company closer to the customer? First of all, by insisting that managers at all levels visit with customers to learn how they can best be served. Second, by educating customers, particularly by publicizing the application of the company's products in the trade press.

For a young, emerging company, finding those most able to spend the necessary time to do all this will probably mean engaging a small and reputable public relations firm to help with the publicity and writing side of such a communications program. A separate PR firm will also be able to assist greatly in the timely distribution of news.

THE ADVERTISING PROGRAM

Given the foundation of a value system, the recognition that communication is reflected in all facets of the company's operations, and the need for an enthusiastic group of employees, the firm can now consider seriously its advertising program. The marketing manager, at this point, must wrestle with five decision areas: dollars, message, media, timing, and measurement. Because an effective campaign, either primary or secondary to some push efforts, is so integral to marketing strategy, there must be a close working relationship between client and agency. Arm's-length relationships don't make much sense! It's a good idea, in this context, to explain completely to the agency your company's marketing strategy and what the advertising campaign is expected to do. Outline, furthermore, the target audience as well as your near-term budgets, growth plans, and market share expectations. And, above all, be sure the agency knows what kind of company you plan to be, the aforementioned basic values.

In short, the agency is your right arm. It is a key part of your marketing department and deserves to know how you think and act. For the small enterprise, as you can well imagine, a good agency can supplement what are limited marketing resources—market research, segment definition and identification, media purchase, pricing research, the determination of particular strategies. But be careful; the marketing strategy is still yours to originate and execute. The agency can assist, but its primary contribution is to transmit the advertising message creatively. Creativity is what you pay for.

One very helpful exercise is to cut out from trade journals and magazines the ads run by competitors that are particularly appealing. This file will help the agency immensely in judging your likes and dislikes. Even more important, be as explicit as possible on the question of budget. If you insist on the highest quality of performance, then you must make it clear that you are willing to pay over and above the standard 15 percent commission. It is unrealistic, particularly for the new firm, to ask an agency to speculate that later they will be properly rewarded for their unprofitable initial efforts. Make it clear at the outset that what the company is after, and what is expected—the very best efforts and brains available in that agency, including but not limited to the senior management.

Some observers feel that advertising and public relations should be separated organizationally for ethical reasons. While this may have validity in some situations, do not overlook the fact that both parties are working toward the same corporate goals. The projects and programs of each should be complementary, not competitive. Indeed, in an emerging company, advertising and public relations should report to the same executive.

Presumably, the primary thrust of the initial advertising will be product. Awareness and sales support are the heart of the advertising mission. This effort to pull sales through the channel of distribution can be effective, particularly if the campaign is fresh and to the point. Moreover, *it is vital that the ad message be supportive of that being delivered in the field. One very good rule to follow: read the ad copy aloud.* Would a sales rep or clerk talking to a prospective customer be embarrassed by the copy, or would the copy enhance and support sales efforts by preconditioning the reader?

Most of us who are not advertising professionals tend to think in terms of print, but the same rules hold true for radio and TV advertising. Another effective medium is the outdoor billboard, which demands a pithy, succinct message.

Since much advertising is subjective, keep in mind that a good agency can provide a quick telephone survey, almost overnight. This means that it is possible to premeasure audience reactions to a planned ad campaign. Trade shows are also a good medium to survey actual buyers for their opinions on brands, product preferences, and other important advertising themes. Surveys, focus groups, and other market research approaches, while somewhat expensive in and of themselves, are often the difference between a successful campaign that really pulls and one that doesn't.

It is also wise to beware of advertising directed to competition or to the company itself. It is a great temptation to speak one's mind in an ad to a competitor who has recently made "close-to-the-bone" claims about reliability or customer satisfaction, or who may even have challenged your product. But remember that no competitor will ever be a good customer. Don't waste your time or talents on the competitor, but concentrate rather on the real buyers of the company's product.

Similarly, the temptation to see your company's own message up there in lights is appealing. Considerable corporate advertising is really intended to impress the friends of the senior executive. There is nothing wrong, however, with a little advertising directed primarily at employees for purposes of morale boosting and inspirational effect. Recognize, however, that this money is being spent for morale, not for sales.

Much attention is given in emerging enterprises to logo types and slogans. But history confirms that many of these were accidentally discovered in the normal course of preparing ads. It is good advice not to spend too much time or money initially on attempting to create the distinctive logo or slogan. Unfortunately, many young companies feel that this is vital and devote precious resources to turning out a "clever" graphic or slogan, which they later regret. Develop an acceptable and attractive layout of the company name initially, and let time take care of the rest. Names rarely make or break a company.

Above all, a communication and advertising program should be fun. It should encourage all hands to participate with ideas and suggestions. Then the product of these efforts should be displayed everywhere, for all to see. Make each employee proud and eager to participate in the future of this enterprise.

MERCHANDISING AND PROMOTION

Though the two are closely allied, and often described interchangeably, it is a reasonable marketing exercise to distinguish merchandising efforts from promotions and deals. Merchandising, as defined earlier, includes the entire range of selling inducements that come into play at the point of purchase. We would include in this definition displays, samples, the store ambience, demonstrations, special packaging, shelf location (particularly in self-service outlets), the width and depth of product line, and the dress and appearance of the employees. Industrial companies make just as much use of merchandising as do consumer goods or service companies. The industrial salesman who gives the latest chip to a design engineer, or refers to company data sheets and technical literature, or takes a prospect on a plant tour, is merchandising.

Merchandising efforts supplement, and enhance, advertising, direct selling, and promotions. In a way, a lot of the best merchandising efforts act as a "silent inducement" to buy—such as the layout of a department store, the internal decor of a fancy dress shop, or the atmosphere in a first-class restaurant. Just contemplate the subtle persuasions that we are exposed to in these carefully merchandised situations!

Promotions

Promotions, normally coupled in conversational usage with "deals," are specific buying incentives addressed to either the consumer or the channel. They are a major part of life in the consumer goods business. Common deals and promotions include, for the channels, display allowances ("Build a display of our product, Mr. Retailer, and we'll pay you x dollars"), advertising allowances, special price packs, and quantity discounts (thirteen for the price of twelve), and, for the consumer, premiums, two-for-the-price-of-one, samples, coupons, price-off packs, contests, and sweepstakes.[3]

There are two commonly cited reasons for spending on promotions: to obtain new and increased distribution, and to provide the consumer with an immediate reason to buy. Promotions are, in the final analysis, price cuts. But there is a vast difference: promotions are viewed as immediate moves that can be tailored to each market situation. Hence the seller feels he has greater control, and certainly flexibility, than if he cut prices across the board.

The more interesting questions are less about promotions in their own right and more about the appropriate balance between promotions and advertising. A preliminary report by the Marketing Services Institute indicated that over the only time period for which they had data, the split between the two categories was as follows:[4]

---

[3] This and the following material adapted from Roger A. Strang, *The Relationship Between Advertising and Promotion in Brand Selling*, Marketing Science Institute, Special Report 75-110, Cambridge, Mass., 1975.

[4] Alden Clayton, *The Relationship between Advertising and Promotion: Some Observations, Speculation and Hypotheses*, Marketing Science Institute, Special Report 75-110, Cambridge, Mass., 1975.

Consumer Goods—$ Spent

	1969	1975	ANNUAL RATE
Sales Promotions	$16.4 billion	$27.9 billion	9.2%
Advertising	$14.6 billion	$19.4 billion	5.0%

You will note by these numbers that promotional expenditures in the consumer markets are larger than advertising, and growing faster. Remember our earlier observations about the value theory—the relevant values are shifting into the channels. Nothing is absolute, however. Advertising and promotional spending together are considered necessary to grow the brands; the key management issues consequently are amount and proportions.

Of particular interest to the marketer is the accelerated swing toward promotions and the fact that most of the promotional growth has been in trade, not consumer, promotions. It is tempting to speculate why:

- Fewer significant product innovations
- Trade pressures: an insistence on promotion programs
- Promotion-minded competitors
- Economy-minded consumers
- Increased acceptance of promotions by top management
- Better-qualified personnel in the promotion function
- The product management system: i.e., emphasis upon short-term results
- Inflation/recession: to dump inventories and increase cash flows
- Development of effective new promotion techniques (in ad coupon, computer sampling, better testing services available)
- Government restrictions on advertising, such as with cigarettes and children's TV

Suppliers of packaged consumer goods are more than casually interested in this swing because there is reason to believe that the well-being of brands is a function of the advertising/promotion mix. The argument is made that strong consumer brand attitudes create a loyal base of committed consumers, and such attitudes are dependent upon effective advertising. Deals and promotions, in contrast, have but a transitory impact and, in fact, are more often than not directed at the trade.

Successful brands, by this argument, should have a market share in advertising and profits that exceeds their market share in sales, while less successful brands exceed their market share in share of trade promotions and deals and fall below in respect to advertising and profits.

There seem to be a number of variables that influence the mix of promotions and advertising. Consider the following:

Influencing Variables

MORE RELATIVE ADVERTISING	MORE RELATIVE PROMOTION
High profits (to support the campaign)	Late in life cycle
Brand awareness	Impulse purchase
Customer values not obvious	High obsolescence or perishability risk
Domination of the market	Strong retail brands
A planned purchase	

The subject of deals and promotions is treated in a cavalier manner by many managements. Compared with advertising controls, promotions are loosely handled. An unpublished teaching note on this subject, written by one of the authors, provides a summary of the more prevalent attitudes about advertising and promotions derived from a number of sources:

1. Company marketing plans are surprisingly short term in focus, e.g., "last year modified."

2. Advertising and promotions are seldom coordinated—in fact different personnel typically handle each.

3. There is a scarcity of information about promotional costs and cannibalization effects.

4. Promotions are expensive: a $1 allowance with a $3 contribution requires a sales increase of 50 percent: $2 would require a doubling of sales.

5. The proper measurement of promotional effectiveness requires "sales against long-term trend," as well as the degree of cannibalization.

6. Promotions are short-lived and seem to be most effective when used sparingly or when coupled with a strong selling and advertising effort and applied to new or fast-growing products.

7. Marginal effectiveness of advertising and promotion varies by markets owing to penetration differences, sales approaches, area demographics, competition, and trade variations.

8. Promotions should not exceed the consumer's average consumption cycle.

9. Promotion effectiveness diminishes when comparable promotions follow too rapidly.

10. Features (e.g., mention in the store's newspaper advertising) have the greatest impact upon sales. But management control over features is weak.

SUMMARY

Communication is the link between buyer and seller. It consists of a large number of tactical variables that are normally defined as selling, advertising, merchandising and promotions, and public relations. The effectiveness of these four depends considerably on their internal fit (are they treated like a system rather than four discrete activities?) as well as management's ability to reinforce the communication message by its public image.

Advertising is designed to influence favorably consumer brand attitudes. As such, its impact is long term. Deals and promotions, by comparison, are short-term inducements and have as much impact on the trade as they do on the consumer.

Merchandising is the umbrella under which the other communication variables operate. The marketing task is to combine all of these communication variables into a persuasive package.

8

Selling

We speculated in the last chapter that many emerging enterprises select personal selling as their first approach to the markets. A bit of advertising may be used to create some general awareness and interest, but the instinctive reliance is upon salespeople, either company-employed or independent, to persuade and induce trial. Whereas good advertising will create awareness, selling converts this awareness into purchases. The power of personal selling is particularly high in the instance of intangibles and products that are complex, service-dependent, expensive, or unique—where trust, confidence, and reliability are significant buying ingredients. Examples would include insurance, investment banking, medical instrumentation, expensive jewelry, computers, and machine tools.

Selling is but one element of the marketing mix, and it is not unusually described as the "implementation" variable. By this reasoning marketing establishes the strategy and sales carries it out. But this assertion is too simplistic and contains two flaws:

1. The real-life complexities and nuances of a sales strategy are buried in the generalization.
2. There are frequently two levels of customers, users and intermediaries (retailers and wholesalers, for example), which demand separate full-fledged strategies.

Returning to the first flaw, the specific actions that lie behind "carrying it out" are quite involved and represent the heart of any sales program.

To illustrate, we have itemized below the decisions sales managers must make:

1. Identifying specific customers (marketing will have defined the segments, but not the accounts)
2. Selecting key accounts
3. Determining key account strategies
4. Defining the role of selling in the marketing strategy
5. Organizing the sales function
6. Deciding the manning needs—how many, doing what, to whom, and where
7. Spelling out the supervisory structure, duties as well as span of control
8. Recruiting and selecting salespeople
9. Training, both horizontal (present job) and vertical (tomorrow's job)
10. Compensating and motivating
11. Evaluating and measuring performance
12. Controlling the results

The sales manager, it can be seen, deals with a wide assortment of operating issues, and not merely some broad execution guidelines suggested by the marketing strategy.

As for the second flaw, in many companies there are two markets— user and intermediary—and the sales force deals with the latter while advertising (primarily) deals with the former. Each market demands its own dedicated strategy. An illustration would be General Foods. Whereas the home office product managers aim their advertising and product plans at the homemaker (the consumer), the sales force concentrates on the needs of the retail and wholesale trades (the customer). Just as consumers have particular product, segment, price, communication, and distribution needs, so, too, do the retailers. As a consequence, the manufacturer's trade activities should be recognized as *industrial* marketing just as his advertising efforts are recognized as *consumer*. So-called consumer goods companies, in this respect, are mislabeled, from a marketing point of view. Hence our concern that "sales carries out the strategy" is a deceptive generalization.

Talking abstractly about salespeople is a further source of difficulty.

There is no prototype, no "average" salesman. Harry R. Tosdal, in his classic volumes on compensation, identifies the following sales variations:[1]

House-to-house canvassing

Selling consumer products of high unit value like automobiles, major appliances, etc., direct to final users

Selling various products like milk, laundry, etc., on retail truck or wagon routes

Selling life insurance

Selling securities or liability, fire, and other forms of insurance

Selling consumer goods on wagon route to retailers for resale, combining delivery, order taking, and other selling functions

Selling grocery or drug products, etc., etc., to retailers and wholesalers for resale on established routes, including in duties routine merchandising service like display help, etc.

Selling to retailers, dealers, or wholesalers combined with missionary or detailing work to induce use, specification, prescription, display, etc.

Primarily "missionary" work to obtain use, specification, display, etc.

Selling specialty consumer products to retailers and wholesalers or distributors for resale, with responsibility for narrow line of products, and emphasis on retail sales program development

General line selling of consumer products to wholesalers and retailers for resale with responsibility for wide product lines

Selling advertising service, space, printing, employment service, and other business services

Selling office equipment, supplies, and similar products requiring technical training for design of systems and installations

Selling equipment, supplies, and materials to hotels, hospitals, restaurants, public institutions, schools

. . . Selling machinery and equipment of high unit value to manufacturers or processors, where chemical, electrical, engineering, etc., knowledge is required for design, installation, and "trouble shooting"

. . . Selling supplies and materials where similar technical knowledge is required to give adequate service

---

[1] Harry R. Tosdal, *Salesmen's Compensation*, Volume I (Boston: Division of Research, Harvard Business School, 1953), pp. 360–361. Reprinted by permission.

Selling industrial equipment, supplies, and materials, where less technical education is required, but great familiarity with trade customs, markets, and personalities is essential

Selling industrial equipment, supplies, and materials to dealers and distributors for resale

Derek Newton, in a more recent study, described four contrasting selling categories:[2]

Trade selling—salesmen try to build sales volume by providing customers with promotional assistance (referred to as "selling through")

Missionary selling—salesmen increase sales by providing direct customers with personal selling assistance (i.e., medical detail men who try to persuade the doctor to prescribe particular brands)

Technical selling—selling is focused on providing technical advice to the direct buyer (such as a computer salesman)

New business selling—cold calling or prospecting

Selling differs along other dimensions as well. There may be a single sales individual or a team. In many complex selling environments, such as AT&T with a large, multidimensioned industrial customer, there are national account teams of forty, fifty, or even one hundred individuals assigned to the one customer. Some team members are generalists and some specialists; some "front line" actors and others "behind the scene"; some commercial in their orientation and others technical. As authors, we have chosen to write primarily in terms of Newton's last two categories, technical and new business selling.

Because selling is so heterogeneous and many-sided, old stereotypes of the traveling salesman are meaningless. Drummers are a disappearing lot. The preferred sales individual today is a professional, not a peddler. He (or she) is expected to know his markets and his products and services, to make a handsome living, and to be a distinct asset to the community. He impacts significantly upon company profits; indeed, it is perfectly reasonable, in many cases, to translate the salesman's results into "earnings per share." Today's selling places a premium on proficiency, energy, creativity, and integrity. Sales success, in other words, is not haphazard. One sales manager, in talking to his local crew, stated, "Your challenge is to control each situation in which

---

[2] Derek Newton, "Get the Most Out of Your Salesforce," *Harvard Business Review*, September–October 1969, pp. 150–163.

you find yourselves. Succeed and your reward will be the thrill of achievement on a recurring basis."

TIME AND TERRITORY MANAGEMENT

The salesperson's scarce resource is time. He or she must, as a critical requirement, plan the sales approach. The plan doesn't have to be elaborate, but it should separately address the tasks to be performed and the priorities as well as "due dates." Initially the plan will be rudimentary, but it will gain in sophistication as the individual develops the essential skills. The entire process is self-reinforcing, and the cumulative experience of the sales individual will make it easier to crack more complicated accounts. By planning specific steps and benchmark milestones needed to complete the sale, the sales individual can juggle several important projects simultaneously without a logjam of paperwork. A simple illustration: One of the authors traveled for several weeks with trade salespeople employed by a major food manufacturer. Each individual finished the separate retail calls by sitting behind the wheel of the car and completing the detailed call report. Elapsed time? About ten minutes for each call, or over one hour each day. All, that is, except for one young lady, who didn't fill out any reports. When asked why, she said, "I filled them out last weekend. All I do now is correct for things I didn't accomplish as planned!" Not surprisingly, most of her calls came out as planned.

Because "hours in the day" are the constraint, time and territory management are an essential aspect of sales planning. How the sales individual covers the territory and allots time distinguishes good from poor performers. In case after case, detailed analysis shows, unfortunately, that too many salespeople spend more of their day traveling and waiting than they do selling. The cost of this waste is enormous and magnifies the importance of high-quality calls. The latest Department of Commerce figures tell us that a person-to-person sales call, on the average, costs between $112.50 and $176.80, including normal travel at 19¢ a mile as well as overhead, salary, and commission. Actually it is far better to think about the value of calls rather than their cost. If the sales individual is planning to earn $50,000, and will need to make between 800 and 1,000 calls in the process, then the value of each call is between $50 and $65. It takes but a moment's reflection to recognize that the true cost of calls is in the bad ones—where, in other words, the seller loses ground or even a sale; where the seller wastes time!

The sophisticated salesperson recognizes the need for account planning, which assumes that for every sale there is a sales cycle. To pass through this cycle to a completed sale, the seller must establish and meet critical milestones. Each milestone leads to the next, and each is the culmination of sales call objectives. Critical milestones must be observable and require customer commitment to action. Hence, "Get the marketing manager's agreement to support our proposal for a sales compensation study" qualifies, whereas "Find out what the manager thinks the major problems are" does not.

How many calls should each salesperson make each day? That depends entirely on such factors as product, size and composition of the territory, customer needs and buying procedures, and size of the average order. If the salesperson is flying to Orlando to call on Disney World, it will be difficult to make two calls that day unless he also has business with Martin Marietta in the same town. By and large, however, in a representative industrial territory, one really has to try hard to make at least three calls daily, and with a little energy that can and should go to four. In sales of packaged consumer goods to food stores, on the other hand, the calls might range from eight to twelve, while a bottler soft drink salesman in Mexico might attain sixty to seventy-five per day (though each sale may only be for two or three bottles to a tiny outlet).

Time is money: professional businesspeople use most lunch periods for contacts. To see an aspiring salesman eating lunch at a drugstore counter because he won't pay for the expense of a business lunch is to see an individual who really has missed the mark in his thinking. Watson of IBM used to wisely admonish his sales force, "Something significant happens in almost every company at least every thirty days." Coverage is the salesperson's principal insurance against surprise from competition, and the major opportunistic tool to take advantage of changes in customer needs. Therefore, the able salesperson must set achievable coverage goals on a daily, weekly, or monthly basis. For example:

2 to 3 personal calls per day

5 initial or follow-up phone calls per day

1 or 2 direct mail pieces or letters sent off daily

Consider what this adds up to weekly:

10–15 personal calls

25 phone calls

5–10 mail items

or monthly:

40–50 calls

100 phone calls

20–30 mail pieces

To achieve the distinction of competent selling requires hard work and practice. But it also takes a lot of common sense and sound instincts. There is no end of perfectly able salespeople who do adequately what they are trained to do. There is a much smaller percentage that have that extra quality of "feel" or "instinct." These are the superstars, the naturals, who probably can't explain what it is that gives them the instinctive edge.

What does the top-flight sales individual do to bring order to a complex territory? First the salesperson inventories his or her assets, both territorial and personal. What does the salesperson bring to the party? What is he or she good at? What needs to be done to better cover this territory—product knowledge, industry specialization, club membership, contacts? Second, the territory—what is in it? Are there useful data about specific customers? What is the present share of market? Which competitor is strongest? Is the product population dense enough to be segmented by industry, application or other classification? If the product requires maintenance, the salesperson must be sure to search out the service people and talk with them about happy customers and past problems that may impede the sale.

It pays to remember at this early stage in the territory that you need help from everyone, and no one needs help from you! Humility goes a long way. You are never wrong by being nice to someone. Take the time to make friends and establish allies. You can also, in these early days, spend time rummaging through files looking for records, cold trails, and existing leads that have not been pursued. Leave no stone unturned.

Lists are helpful. Depending somewhat upon your product, there are all kinds of lists available to the resourceful. Whether one starts with the Yellow Pages or the Fortune 500, computerized lists abound (for example, Lawyers—Corporation, Divorce, Trial, Probate, or Lumberyards—Local, Regional, National, Retail/Wholesale. How about members of the local Chamber of Commerce who gave to the last United Way Appeal or to the latest drive for funds for the performing arts? Such lists can be obtained on computer tape or gummed mailing labels, sorted alphabetically or by such attributes as size, number of employees, annual revenues, standard industrial classification (SIC), or zip code.

The reason for collecting lists may seem obvious, but all too many neophyte salespeople overlook this essential building block of territory management. To succeed, the salesperson must take an inventory of the territorial assets—the people and organizations. Otherwise he'll be like a rat in a maze. "If you don't know where you are going, any road will take you there." Since these lists will be the primary input into the salesperson's business plan, that individual must set up a system that will not only capture the initial information but permit adding names and other data over time.

The new sales recruit will probably find that the predecessor has left a few three-by-five cards and other primitive source data. Hopefully the sales office will have some additional details on past customer and prospect activity. Don't overlook, for example, old accounts-receivable files and invoice lists. The first "not available" reply from clerical should be ignored. Somehow the salesperson must unearth the buying data that lies buried somewhere in the books of the bean counters. The objective is to prepare an account profile for each key prospect and customer which will permit the development of individual account strategy programs.

Needless to say, this process takes time and effort. The data required and their sources are varied. Who buys? Who approves? Who influences? What is this account's buying record? How much will they need? Of what type? Who are the alternative suppliers? How much business have the competitors sold? What is the competitor's edge? Who are the competitor's chief contacts within the buying firm?

Where to look? There are many possibilities: other customers, the competitors (salespeople love to talk), your own company records, the local library, reference volumes such as Standard and Poor's or Dun and Bradstreet's as well as the customer's annual reports and 10Ks.

Why go to all this trouble? So you can call prepared! You will never look up a company or executive reference without learning at least one thing helpful in determining the right approach to use, the anecdote to tell, or the reference name to drop.

The newly assigned salesperson will find it useful to call at least one level above that of his or her predecessor. It is only old naval courtesy to ask the existing contact if he can arrange for you to pay your respects to the boss or the president. In short, make the most of what is really your honeymoon stage.

Many salespeople find it advantageous to ask for a plant tour—how else can you so readily see how the account uses your product and competitive products? On such tours, additionally, there are innumerable opportunities to ask about neighboring firms that might be potential customers, or customer's problems that your firm might solve. After all, you are the nice sales individual who has shown a sincere interest in their firm! It pays to be courteous, for example, by sending a short note, along with an interesting reprint or a topical book.

By this time the neophyte has a pretty good grasp of the territory. He knows each account's needs, potential buying patterns, internal policies, critical personnel, and competitive inroads. This knowledge facilitates the next stage, that of estimating sales for the next three, six, twelve, or more months. One unusual but effective technique is to use the "rule of twenty." (These figures will certainly change by situation.) Identify the twenty top prospects or underdeveloped customers in the territory that can be closed within six months. You may or may not be able to sell them all, but you should at least be in the running. And the chase will keep you in first-class sales condition.

Prospecting, for the competent salesperson, is exciting. A salesperson who doesn't enjoy calling on a complete stranger to try to sell him something he doesn't recognize he needs, will never truly succeed. If you know your product and have pride in it, if you have confidence in your persuasive ability, and if you are willing to work hard to explain the merits of your company and products, then you should enjoy going out and doing the missionary work so necessary to developing and harvesting a territory.

Remember the famous World Series game between Philadelphia and Kansas City in 1980? Bases loaded, last of the ninth, score tied, two out. The catcher goes out to the mound to talk with the pitcher, who subsequently strikes out the batter. Later a sportswriter asked the catcher what he said to the pitcher to settle him down at the crucial moment.

The catcher replied, "Isn't it exciting?" You have arrived in selling, to use another baseball analogy, if with bases loaded, last of the ninth, two outs, and a one-run lead, you say, "I hope he hits it to me!"

Prospecting presents the ideal opportunity to try new approaches, to experiment with new openers, closes, trial closes, and other presentation techniques. Prospecting provides an easy way to practice without much risk of damaging valuable customer relationships.

One way to prospect is to "shotgun" everything in sight. But that entails a hideous waste—hot prospects are mixed with impossible ones, and the salesperson blows a lot of time. So it helps to use your lists to classify possible calls by industry or business type. Such preparation and forethought make it possible for the seller to build up specific industry solutions and product applications. Moreover, by selecting just a few names from a larger classified array, the sales individual can make some trial runs. If, for example, one product in the line has an application in banks, then the salesperson should make a short list of banks and pick out one that is a reasonable-seeming candidate, on the basis perhaps of size, volume, and available buyer information. He should research the name to call on and then make the call. He should not go off with wild enthusiasm and make the initial bank call on the biggest and best. Remember, selling is a game, and games are played to be won.

So much of selling is asking the right questions. It is knowing enough about the other fellow's problems that you can effectively probe, learn, and gain some confidence. And if you make an early sale, that's great. Or perhaps you will pick up a useful lead. Do you, for example, have the audacity, having called on the fourth best prospect on your banking list—say, Fourth National Bank—to ask at the end of the interview if the person you are calling on knows Mr. Jackson at the Third National Bank? If so, does he think Mr. Jackson would be interested in what you are selling? You have heard about making your own leads and perhaps have wondered what referral selling was. If you try that last suggestion, you will be in the heart of referral selling.

Once the new sales individual has scouted the territory, he should think about the quality of his call schedule. Quantity of calls is no substitute for quality. As a case in point, if you start your calls at the bottom, you'll never make it to the top. Many studies have compared successful and unsuccessful salespeople. It is frequently found, and particularly in the case of high-ticket items, that the number-one differentiation between the good and the bad is the ability to sell at the top. Even though the purchasing department is an important element in the buying process, senior management usually plays a role proportionate to the price or importance of the purchase.

Why do so many salespeople fail to tell their story at a high enough level? A number of explanations come to mind:

- Lack of self-confidence
- Officer/enlisted-man syndrome
- Not equipped socially
- Unprepared at a business level
- Awestruck

There are lots of ways to call successfully on senior managers. How about the following: (1) Do your homework so that you can adapt your product and other benefits to the specific concerns of the manager being addressed. (2) Ask questions, and listen a lot. (3) Learn to describe your business and the purpose of your call quickly. (4) Act natural. The individual who projects what he or she really is—not some artificial robot—is respected and listened to. (5) Remember that the senior manager is not "somehow different." As the old saying goes, "He puts on his pants one leg at a time." What's the worst thing that could happen to you in front of this executive? He won't hit you or physically throw you out of his office. Quite the contrary. He won't try to publicly embarrass you. (6) Look the part. Appearances do make a difference. The following survey of buyers is to the point and was reported by the Research Institute of America.

	YES	NO
1. On a salesman's first call, are you very much aware of his appearance?	98.0%	2.0%
2. Does your awareness of his appearance diminish with succeeding calls?	39.0	61.0
3. Do you form a definite opinion of a salesman from his appearance?	57.0	43.0
4. Is your inclination to listen affected by:		
his dress?	56.5	43.5
his grooming?	73.0	27.0

	YES	NO
5. Would you tend to judge the company by the salesman's appearance?	82.5	17.5
6. Do you like or expect to receive a business card from a businessman?	95.5	4.5
7. Do you like a salesman's appearance to reflect the latest fashion in dress and grooming?	27.5	72.5
8. Would you like to see him traditionally or conservatively well dressed?	74.0	26.0
9. Do you normally notice such things as:		
soiled or wrinkled clothing?	84.5*	15.5
badly tied tie?	58.0*	42.0
unshined shoes?	63.5*	36.5
run-down heels?	40.0*	60.0
five-o'clock shadow?	61.5*	38.5
chewed fingernails?	42.0*	58.0
clashing colors?	41.5*	58.5

	OK	NOT OK
10. How do you feel about:		
a beard?	55.5%	44.5%
long hair (below tips of ears)?	29.5	70.5
cigar smoking?	60.0	40.0
gum chewing?	38.0	62.0

*Negative reaction
Adapted from Research Institute of America, "Sales Action Coordinator," 1974.

In other words, act the part.

SUMMARY

Selling is very much an activity of marketing, but it has its own strategic requirements. Suppliers that sell through distributors and dealers have two strategic targets, the trade and the user. The sales force is both the architect of channel strategy and executor of the user strategy.

Because time is the scarce resource, the sales force must practice time and territory management; such planning is essential to effective selling. Perhaps the most critical time period in this regard is the initial month or two. This is when data are collected and plans formulated. There are a number of simple rules about data gathering and prospecting that successful salespeople have used over the years. Perhaps the best advice that can be given to a new sales individual is the following:

1. Be yourself.
2. Sell the benefits.
3. Call in depth.
4. Listen.
5. Remember that buyer confidence is the critical variable.

9

Sales Management

Our discussion of selling is but half the loaf: the other half is supervision. The success or failure of the individual salesperson is very much the result of the competence of management. Strong managers develop strong salespeople; weak ones do not. This is hardly a surprising observation—it is substantiated in much of the research—and its essence is captured succinctly in the following hypothetical conversation between a field sales manager and a friend:

Sales manager: My salesmen are sure lousy.

Friend:　　　 Who selected them?

Sales manager: I did.

Friend:　　　 Who trained them?

Sales manager: I did.

Friend:　　　 Who supervises them?

Sales manager: I do.

Friend:　　　 Who's lousy?

The dependence of the field sales force upon the sales manager is the result of the peculiar nature of the selling job. In comparison to other positions in the company:

1. The salesperson usually operates individually and experiences the thrills and disappointments of the sales calls alone. His or her emotional ups and downs are pronounced; a competent manager is needed to help level the emotional roller coaster.

2. The sales individual sets his own pace and decides whether to

start work at eight or nine in the morning, to quit at five or six or to skip certain calls. It's difficult to set your own pace over time. Strong supervision ensures effective work habits.

3. The salesperson, as stated earlier, along with the field supervisor, is the company's local representative. Quality control, through management, is essential given this leverage.

4. The successful individual is not a particularly sensitive self-critic. Can you imagine a star performer who says, "I'm the world's worst"? Quite the contrary: the salesperson's makeup leads to the opposite conclusion: "I'm the world's best!" That's fine for generating morale and enthusiasm, but it doesn't help the sales individual to recognize personal shortcomings. Good supervision helps to generate that insight.

The task of the sales manager is complicated by the fact that the salespeople are scattered; sales management is a job of remote supervision. There is not the satisfaction, or practical supervisory advantage, of seeing, touching, and reaching each subordinate once every day or, for that matter, as often as necessary. Aside from the basic supervisory task of overseeing work habits and comportment that "within-view" management facilitates, remoteness makes it more difficult to engender high morale, loyalty, and dedication to the firm and product.

The normal solution to this problem of separation is to rely on a field sales manager—supervisor, branch manager, district manager, or regional manager. These functionaries are the sales manager's surrogates. Surprisingly, there is probably no more ignored group in marketing than the local managers. They are all too often expected to acquire their supervisory skills by osmosis. "You were an outstanding salesman. No reason you can't manage!"

Nothing, unfortunately, could be further from the truth. Selling encourages individual performance; management focuses on "the team." Selling is based on persuasion, management upon involvement, teamwork, and leadership. Selling is mostly doing with some planning; management is mostly planning with some doing. The jobs are not intellectually incompatible, but they certainly call for different attitudes, skills, and behaviors.

An earlier study isolated five functions ordinarily assumed by local managers.[1] First is the requirement to develop the sales force, including

---

[1] Robert T. Davis, *Performance and Development of Field Sales Managers* (Boston: Harvard University, Division of Research, Graduate School of Business, 1957).

recruiting and selecting as well as coaching and training. Next the supervisory task, which includes controlling and motivating the sales force. Third, there is personal selling. Not all field managers sell, to be sure, but despite the many heated arguments pro and con, a great many do. Administering a field office is the fourth essential field management duty. Finally, there is the manager's responsibility for effectively wearing the trappings of office—the local title and prestige of authority.

Sales management, needless to say, assumes the existence of a sales force. We shall, accordingly, next address the question of where the sales force comes from in those cases where management elects to hire its own.

RECRUITING AND SELECTING

The sales manager's major investment decision is the sales force. What does one salesperson cost to hire and develop? It wouldn't be out of line to speculate that, assuming a six-month learning period, the direct costs of the individual would exceed $40,000 (pay for six months plus fringes and back-up support), not to mention lost sales during the break-in period. Or taking a broader view, let's estimate the value of a competent sales individual over a normal career. How about ten or twenty times the annual take-home plus fringes?

What are the initial steps facing the sales manager in this manning effort? To start with, there needs to be a job description. What are the requirements of the selling job, both duties and behavior? This document represents the contract between salesperson and company. It spells out the salesperson's work, for which the company is prepared to pay an annual sum. The job description is the applicant's first evidence, moreover, that the position does, or does not, meet his or her expectations.

Once the job description is in hand the manager should convert the requirements into a "spec sheet." What kind of individual is preferred? What is the profile of the most suitable candidate? Although the jump from job description to profile is tenuous, the try can help to eliminate a good number of questionable applicants. It follows, of course, that both job description and personal specifications will alter over time.

For the neophyte sales manager there are a number of questions that are well worth considering:

1. Is the job description consistent with reality? It's all too easy to "oversell" the candidate, who discovers after the fact that what he anticipated didn't match the actual. Result? A turnover of one!

2. Can the applicant grow, not only vertically (that is, into higher jobs) but horizontally (into a more complex version of the current position)? This is a tough one to predict, but more than one manager has regretfully discovered that three or four years later the sales force contained a number of unresponsive duds. This is doubly embarrassing if the manager had originally hired some friends and past associates.

3. Is the applicant smart? Hungry? Does he or she have integrity? These three show up regularly on most managers' "want lists."

4. Does the candidate have the instincts of a natural salesperson? Competent selling is a potpourri of experience, training, desire, and instincts. The instincts are invaluable, probably can't be taught, and act like a special antenna for the fortunate possessor (e.g., "It feels right?" "I have a hunch," "This may be wild, but . . .").

5. Has the applicant been successful at anything?

6. Has the manager made the final selections from a large enough pool? It's a recurring weakness for sales managers to choose from eight or ten rather than from fifty or sixty. With numbers obviously comes the increased possibility of finding stars.

7. Does the applicant like to sell? to prospect? to make the tough calls?

How does the manager unearth such information? The applicant's history (the application blank) will supply a number of hints. Is he or she a job hopper? Does the individual have a record of steady improvement (jobs and compensation)? What has the applicant accomplished that is noteworthy? Is there any unreported time interval in the résumé?

A second source (the personal interview) should be a useful indicator of potential. But the trick is to set up the interview questions so as to elicit such insight. For example, "How would you react to the following situation . . . ?" "What is there about this job that you most like?" "What are you really good at?" It helps, in addition, to have several managers participate in the interviewing so that the interviewers can pool their impressions.

Recommendations from past employers are of some, but limited, value. Most employers, for good reason, are unwilling to put their honest opinions in writing. The best way to beat this reluctance is to telephone or even pay a personal visit. Phone conversations are less threatening to the recommender and allow the hiring manager to probe for some specifics about the more difficult-to-judge personal attributes.

Tests are used in a number of companies, but their usefulness is seriously debated. The following quotation sums up the questionable nature of this approach:[2]

> The limited empirical work investigating the effects of sales aptitude on performance is summarized in Ghiselli's review of the predictive validity of various aptitude tests. He reports relatively high average validity coefficients between sales performance criteria and two types of aptitude tests: (1) test of intellectual abilities (.31) and (2) tests of personality traits (.27). Though the relationships between these kinds of aptitude tests and performance are stronger for salespeople than for persons in many other occupations, the two types of aptitude measures considered together as independent predictors still cannot explain more than 17% of the variance in sales performance.

There are, to be sure, other kinds of tests—intelligence, manual dexterity, and preferences, to cite a few. Regardless of the type employed, most protagonists of tests caution that they should be used only as a supplementary selection aid. As such, the tests may provide some useful ideas; at least they can provide leads for further investigation.

Finally in the recruiting process is the question of where the sales manager turns to find applicants. There are a number of commonly used sources:

- Customers: Who do they view as strong salespeople among their suppliers?

- Salespeople: Your own employees can help, and they are familiar with the environment.

- Other company employees: This sometimes works because you have the advantage of knowing the applicant. Unfortunately, more often than not, such employees probably don't have the necessary desire to sell; otherwise they would already have done so.

- Recent graduates: This pool has the advantage of providing fresh, "unspoiled" talent. These graduates have not been prejudiced by earlier selling jobs.

---

[2] O. C. Walker, G. A. Churchill, Jr., and N. M. Ford, "Motivation and Performance in Industrial Selling: Present Knowledge and Needed Research," *Journal of Marketing Research*, May 1977, pp. 156–168.

- Advertisements: The media can dredge up many inquiries. And that's the problem. The challenge is to word the job description and personnel requirements in such a way as to discourage the marginal candidates from applying.

- Placement agencies: OK for many positions, but these agencies are not likely to screen carefully unless you make specific arrangements in advance.

- Drop-ins: If the sales manager keeps a current file on drop-ins it is always possible that there are several names currently available.

TRAINING

Training, when stripped of its conventional trappings, deals fundamentally with "changing behavior." Otherwise, there would be no reason for it. A useful starting point, therefore, is to evaluate those influences that alter selling behavior. We have identified seven:

Knowledge about the product and technology

Knowledge about customers, the territory, the organization, and competition

Selling skills

Work habits

Attitudes

Personality

Intelligence

We can conveniently drop the last two in our discussion of training because they are largely fixed by the time the salesperson is hired. We can't do much about changing them. They are accordingly more relevant as recruiting and selecting criteria.

But the others can be changed, and this process of alteration is what training is all about. Training, we can see, is more than imparting knowledge and selling skills; it includes establishing attitudes and work habits. We should be concerned, as trainers, with the entire set.

Who, it is reasonable to ask, is most responsible for orchestrating these influences, for training the sales force?

First and foremost, it is obvious, is the individual trainee. Without personal desire there can be no learning. Imagine the trainee who says to you, "Here I am. Develop me!"

What other training "agents" are there, once we accept the need for a willing student? Several come to mind: the line manager, a staff individual(s) (e.g., a trainer), customers, and peers. Training should allow for the influence of each; each helps to modify behavior. Nonetheless, when all is said and done, one agent stands out as preeminent, the *line manager*. The sales force's attitudes and work habits will, for sure, mirror those of the supervisor. Except for periodic "shots" of formal training, selling skills and product knowledge will develop essentially through the ongoing efforts of the sales manager. Training is not a periodic occurrence; it is an ongoing interaction between salesperson and supervisor. Training is the guts of the manager's job.

A number of tried and true training techniques are available to line management. At the head of the list, most would agree, is that of management behavior itself. The sales force, as with any group, will be responsive to their line supervisors—what the supervisors say, how they act, their attitudes. It is in this sense that it can be said, accurately, that managers cannot escape their training responsibilities.

In the more conventional training sense, a second useful technique is role playing. In role playing the participants act out various salesman/customer scenarios. The participants learn by doing and criticizing. During these sessions the trainees are reminded that effective selling is premised upon the acronym FAB—features, advantages, and benefits. Take the example of your clothing. "Have you noticed the stitching in the lapels?" (Feature). "We stitch all suit jacket lapels because this guarantees that the lapel lies flat and doesn't curl" (Advantage). "So you never have to worry about your appearance" (Benefit).

Commercial training vendors offer a wide assortment of formal sales training programs. In addition, most sales managers supplement these special programs with in-house talent, particularly in respect to imparting product knowledge and product changes.

Training, needless to say, can be less formal. Some takes place in the field, some in group meetings. The common characteristics are flexibility and adaptability. On-the-job coaching (i.e., direct observation) and curbstone critiques are two that have proved popular over the years. In these approaches, the relationship between manager and sales individual is one-on-one and the feedback immediate. Another technique is that of special assignments ("Develop a key account strategy," "Determine the potential of this product," "Compare the different strategies of our competitors"). Such tasks can add a new dimension to the salesperson's perspective, as can "filling in" for an absent manager.

One of the most successful techniques, and therefore one that we shall now elaborate upon, is sales meetings.

SALES MEETINGS

Because new young companies have little past practice to build upon, it is important that frequent meetings be held. So much of the company is in the formative stage that there is considerable room for misunderstanding. Indeed, in such a company, policy decisions frequently emerge from evolving circumstances, for this is the most direct and effective way of meeting difficulties and preventing their recurrence. For example, a hastily put-together brochure and spec sheet might be discovered to be incorrect in some critical aspects after they have been mailed to a prime list. Or tentative pricing might be tried on a highly competitive bid in a new market. If successful, should this policy be adopted as company policy, or should it be abandoned? The answers to these kinds of questions can be formulated most effectively through frank discussion in an open meeting.

The manager should hold informal meetings often, since the grapevine is stronger in an emerging company because of less formal, structured communication. The manager should deliberately set the tone and spirit and lay the groundwork for establishing the winning attitude. Simultaneously, participants will learn together about product, competition, features, advantages, and benefits—and what needs to be done to establish the company and products in the market at a profit. And, of course, each meeting is an opportunity to teach and to train.

So many sales managers say, "Yes, I'd love to have sales meetings, but I don't know what to cover. I don't have anything to talk about, and I don't have the time." But the problem is that there is so much to talk about, and so much to cover, that a manager must make the time.

Sales meetings should be held at least weekly. They can be run by conference, by telephone, or face to face. They can have two or one hundred participants. It does not matter what or to whom the company is selling, but meetings are worth their weight in gold. The effectiveness of such meetings is demonstrated in the following examples.

George Patterson, legendary builder of United Airlines, had a daily morning telephone conference-call with his top managers scattered in Chicago, Denver, Los Angeles, San Francisco, and New York. The question was always the same: "What happened yesterday and what are we going to do to (a) prevent it happening again or (b) see that we continue such good performance?" The answers were obtained by asking who was responsible and who would report back tomorrow morning. Patterson's lieutenants called them "prayer meetings," or "whose turn in the box?," but actually they were sales meetings designed to find out how to serve the customer better.

When Remington Rand bought UNIVAC in 1952, IBM was caught flat-footed, with nothing but spirit to fight off a competitor capable of mortally damaging its punched card business. T. V. Learson, a very tough and able vice-president of sales, called his regional managers in for a sales meeting on what to do. During the morning Thomas Watson (age seventy-seven) came into the room and listened intently. As they broke for lunch he asked Vince Learson if he might say something after lunch. When they reconvened, his chauffeur was in front of the room holding what appeared to be a large painting. The painting was covered with a lap robe from Watson's car. Watson then told of the wild horses in the Far West who had horse sense. (Horse sense, he allowed, was what kept horses from betting on men.) Removing the lap robe, he revealed a Thomas Leigh painting of a dramatic scene in which a group of wild horses in deep snow have made a circle of their lethal hoofs and are defending themselves against an attack by a pack of hungry wolves. Because of the manner in which they have arranged themselves, there is no room for the wolves to attack without being kicked. Watson went on to say, "In winter in the heavy snows, the wolves found that they could easily pull down even a large horse by attacking in unison from all sides. The horses learned that by putting their heads together they could form an impenetrable circle which protected them effectively from the marauding wolves. You managers have been spending the morning talking about the other fellow and your competition. Why not put your heads together and figure out what *his* competition should be?" This dramatic and unforgettable incident served to turn the discussion into a more positive channel, and out of it came the sales strategy which enabled IBM not only to hold the fort against UNIVAC, but eventually to walk away with "all the marbles."

And in the 1950s the Waldorf Astoria was considered the *ne plus ultra* of style and class for grand dinners in New York City. The ambience, elegance, decor, and service were unmatched. Most of the affairs held there were black-tie, and the sight of 2,500 beautifully groomed ladies and gentlemen dining and listening to a distinguished speaker was well remembered. From a marketing point of view, the banquet manager and his staff were thoroughly professional. With great skill they helped the amateur hosts of each occasion plan the menu, seating, flowers, program, and timing within meaningful budgetary restraints. It was well done. But the real difference between the Waldorf and the Plaza or the Astor was Oscar, the maître d'hôtel. His personal income in tips from satisfied clients was a whispered legend. He was everywhere, a battlefield commander: tough, demanding, expecting excellence. This *was* the Waldorf. Woe betide the poor busboy, dishwasher, waiter, or chef's helper who forgot what was expected of him. Just before each major event Oscar held a "sales meeting." All hands crowded into the space available. A quick inspection was held for dress and grooming, followed by instant correction, and then a brief statement describing what the affair was, who were the important attendees, and what special attention or events were needed. Oscar ended with an exhortation to remember the proud tradition each staff member represented that night. It was simple and effective.

The Waldorf may seem a far cry from an IBM meeting or a telephone conference call. However, in these cases two important activities were being accomplished at the same time. First, the bond between the staff and the organization was being reaffirmed. Second, a hard look was being taken at setbacks or mistakes, and the meeting was turned into a learning experience. Remember that there is no managerial substitute for the sales meeting for accomplishing these purposes.

INCENTIVES

Rewards are most certainly an essential management tool. Whether the individual earns and receives one or doesn't has direct impact upon his or her behavior and performance. Furthermore, the size of the reward is, in a direct way, the score card by which the salesperson can assess how management rates him or her.

Rewards can be nonmonetary. Peer ranking is perhaps the single least expensive and yet strongest motivator. A monthly ranking of the sales force is a great stimulator. Additionally, there is a surprising number of nonmonetary incentives available. The range of opportunities for showering pins, buttons, badges, and medals on people is staggering. Some companies believe in special awards, but use them exclusively to honor the top few. Much more vital are the ribbons, news items, and pictures that convey a good show by the common employee of the company. In well-managed concerns it is a badge of distinction to receive such recognition. Nonetheless, the ongoing motivator is cash. And selling is a business activity that is peculiarly suited to monetary rewards. Creative selling isn't accomplished by routine; it calls for ingenuity, varied approaches, and enormously hard work. Hence the salesperson's output has wide bounds that can be greatly influenced by motivation.

Except in those cases where salespeople are primarily order takers, or part of a complex selling team, we prefer to pay 30 or 40 percent of the salesperson's take-home as an incentive, with the rest as salary. However, there are three conditions that should be met before the sales force is challenged by a hefty incentive pay plan:

1. The salesperson's contribution to the sale, even if less than 100 percent, can be identified and measured.

2. There is competent field sales management in place because no incentive plan can replace strong supervision.

3. The sales force is hired with the expectation and knowledge that the carrot will be large (some highly educated, technical salespeople don't want to be viewed as "salesmen on commission").

There are three inputs to an equitable compensation plan: (1) the expected take-home pay for an average performer; (2) the identification and weighting (on a scale of 100) of the sales jobs to be performed (and for which the rewards will be paid); and (3) the various incentive alternatives that might be employed. The accompanying table depicts these three, in a hypothetical situation:

Selling Tasks and Weights

	Prospect	Maintain	Provide Service	Gather Competitive Intelligence	
	50%	25%	15%	10%	Average Pay Expected
Salary					
Commission					
Bonus					↓
Contests					
Liberal expenses					
Other					
Monetary Value	$15,000	$7,500	$4,500	$3,000	$30,000

One could play around with this simple model, but it includes as is the necessary ingredients for preparing a compensation plan. How does it work?

Assuming an average pay (far right) of $30,000, the separate selling jobs are worth $15,000, $7,500, $4,500, and $3,000. But what form should the incentive payment take: salary, commission, bonuses, or what? The answer is to isolate each task and ask, "How many of the dollars that I'm willing to pay for this task, should I pay by salary, commission, contest, or whatever?" Certainly, there is no pat answer, but at least the necessary inputs are considered. The selected plan will undoubtedly represent some simplification of the manager's first dollar allocation, which is likely to be too involved.

QUOTAS

A separate but correlative aspect of incentive schemes is that of quotas and goals. How should they be determined and utilized?

The process begins with the manager's analysis of each territory, which requires a calculation of profit and loss for each. Only when these figures have been identified can a value be assigned to each territory and the expected level of performance defined. Gross costs are typically easy to find. Figures are normally available at the "take-home W-2" level to indicate what a typical salesperson earns. But how about secondary costs such as benefits, travel and entertainment and the cost of support in office space, and clerical help? The accumulated sum is usually impressive and should be reviewed at least yearly. At any rate, given the cost per sales individual, it is then possible, and necessary, to determine how much the rep must sell in order to break even. Break-even is the absolute minimum quota he or she can carry.

To illustrate, if a sales individual expects to earn $50,000 yearly, the sales manager, as a rule of thumb, should double that figure to allow for other costs, or a total of $100,000. For the sales individual to profitably represent the company with a product that carries a 30 percent margin at the field sales level, he or she must bring in approximately $335,000 ($100,000 ÷ 0.30) to reach break-even. (Anything less than $500,000, in fact, is probably of questionable value.) We now have a base point for determining quotas.

The setting of annual quotas is good management practice and is usually linked to the compensation plan, though there are quota systems—for example, where the sales force is on salary—that are in-dependent of compensation. Regardless, the manager must make it clear that quotas are a serious measurement technique, for both management and the individual. Depending upon how they are determined, the quotas help to rank the individual performers, or, if calculated differently, they become valuable personnel development instruments. This last point deserves some explanation.

Quotas are based either on experience (what the individual has done) or potential (what the individual might do), or some combination of the two. The implications of using experience or potential as the base are intriguing. Imagine a two-person sales force with the following performance:

	SALES LAST YEAR (% OF TOTAL SALES)	POTENTIAL SALES (IN RELATIVE PERCENTAGE)	QUOTA FOR NEXT YEAR
Salesperson A	60%	50%	?
Salesperson B	40%	50%	?

Salesperson A, at least on the surface, appears to have done the better job since potential has been exceeded. (Again, let's make some simple assumptions and consider the two territories equal in all respects except number of customers; that is, they are not different in respect to competition, geography, and industry structure.) We shall define potential in its normal sense, as the relative difference in possible sales between the two territories. Typically the information about potential is obtained by comparing the number of presumed sales indicators in each territory—smokestacks if we are selling smokestack cleaner, houses if we are selling window screens. (Obviously these raw figures can be considerably refined; we are trying here only to make a simple point.)

Given these data, how do we set the quota for next year? Do we weight for experience or for potential? The decision affects the two salespeople quite differently. If the quota is determined by experience, then A, the stronger, will receive a higher target than if the quota is based on potential. But the weaker salesperson obtains the opposite results. This can be easily illustrated:

	QUOTA	
	If Based on Experience	If Based on Potential
Salesperson A	higher	lower
Salesperson B	lower	higher

A motivational issue is raised. Do we use the same formula in setting quotas (in order to ensure equity), or do we manipulate the calculation in order to stretch each individual? One would argue for the second approach if individual development is the quota objective. It is better, in other words, for each to be in the "higher" category even though the calculation is different for the separate sales individuals.

Managers, not surprisingly, approach this decision in a pragmatic way. They generally expect more production each year from the same territory covered by the same individual. They argue that the competent representative should have more satisfied customers, more knowledge of who the decision makers are, and where the business is located. Obviously, if several large plants have closed or relocated, a special circumstance has developed that should be treated as such, but the rule of constantly increasing sales is normally followed. "Raise the bar each year and expect it to be cleared" is the philosophy. Where there are several large accounts in a territory—for example, downtown Manhattan or Chicago—and there are several salespeople covering that area, it can be revealing to reassign those accounts on which there has been no visible change in volume during the preceding year. Give these accounts to another salesperson to see what he or she can do. This keeps things from getting stale, and the results are sometimes spectacular. Needless to say, the realization on the part of the sales staff that this can happen is a further stimulant to better coverage and creative salesmanship.

But this philosophy introduces an age-old argument centering on "equitable treatment" among the salespeople. Do we step in when a salesperson is doing poorly with a customer and reassign that account, or do we encourage the sales individual to experiment, keep at it, and learn from the experience? If a poll were taken, we would guess that expediency rules—the account will be reassigned despite the longer-term personnel development costs. The position would be taken that the company owns the territory and leases it to the sales force for rent called "quota."

A CASE STUDY

We could write endless words about the manager's job, but an understanding of *how* the able manager accomplishes that job would be more practical. Several years ago one of the authors had occasion to observe in detail a sales manager attempting to heal a very sick operation. His behavior was exemplary, and his results were superb. Even though he was but one manager in one situation, we think it is worth studying his profile and noting his behavioral skills. The original write-up of this study is reproduced below.[3]

A SALES MANAGER IN ACTION

The Setting The Andrews Food Company manufactured a full line of packaged consumer goods. The annual sales volume of $400 million was distributed directly (40 per cent) and through food wholesalers (60 per cent) to food stores in the United States. A sales force of 200 operated out of 20 branch offices and was expected: (1) to sell direct to the largest retail outlets; (2) to sell through wholesalers to smaller outlets; (3) to service individual stores, including rotating the stock, building displays, checking prices, revamping shelves, packing up "spoils," and so on.

Ordinarily, selling was based upon the presentation of dealer promotions, usually every six weeks. Although Andrews supported a substantial national advertising program, the critical determinant in getting the order was believed to be the extensive retailer promotion program. Retailer promotions included buying allowances, display allowances, advertising allowances, and label packs. Company expenditures for promotions were approximately the same as for national advertising. Both types of expenditures were controlled by brand managers at the home office. Each of the 8 brand managers was accountable for profits in his line. Acceptance of the various promotions by the

---

[3] Robert T. Davis, "A Sales Manager in Action," Readings in Sales Management, ed. Robert T. Davis and Harper Boyd (Homewood, Ill.: Richard D. Irwin, 1970), pp. 259–268.

retailers depended upon several variables including the attractiveness of the offer relevant to competitive offers, past relationships, the retailers' inventory situation, and the selling ability of the field sales force.

The brand managers reported to the marketing vice president through a merchandising manager. The salesmen, on the other hand, reported to the marketing vice president through branch managers, area managers, and a national sales manager. The brand sector was, in effect, the inside "merchandising" group; the sales sector took care of the execution.

This case study centers on an intensive investigation of two managers, one described by senior executives as "our best branch manager," the other as "the worst." The performance records of the two men supported these descriptions:

PERFORMANCE CRITERIA (DURING PAST 16 QUARTERS)	BEST MANAGER	WORST MANAGER
1. Quota attained	15 out of 16 quarters	6 out of 16 quarters
2. Change in market share	Increase from 2% to 11%	Decrease from 12% to 11%
3. Annual rate of salesman turnover	None—except for promotion to better jobs	50%

Top management concurred that the environmental conditions in the two branches were about the same. The difference in results, therefore, was presumably brought about by the local personnel (including the manager).

Because the weaker manager was within two years of retirement, The Andrews Company chose to retire him immediately. The "best" manager was moved into the "worst" manager's branch. During his first 12 months on the new assignment, the strong manager accomplished the following: quota was made in four consecutive quarters (in two of them, the branch was No. 1 in the United States), and market share increased 20 percent. These gains were made, moreover, with a minimum of changes in personnel. One sales individual (out of 17) was fired, one key account manager (out of 2) was dismissed, and one supervisor (out of 2) was promoted to branch manager in another part of the country. How did the manager bring about such a remarkable improvement in the branch in such a few months? What was his behavior?

Examining Behavior Behavior can be categorized into four parts:

1. *Activities.* How does the manager spend his time? What relative importance does he place upon his various tasks?
2. *Sentiments or attitudes.* How does the manager talk about himself and his job? His salesmen? His customers? His competition? Higher management?
3. *Interactions.* With whom does the manager interact, and what role does he play?
4. *Decisions.* What kinds of decisions does the manager make, and on what basis are the decisions made?

The Behavior of the Good Manager

Activities During the year under study, the branch manager spent 55 percent of his time in the field (where he worked primarily with his account managers in key retail outlets) and 45 percent in the office (dealing with competitive analyses and recommendations to the region for special deals and promotions, planning strategy for major blocs of business, and organizational problems). Specifically, the manager allocated his 250 working days as follows:

71 days (28%) with account managers

60 days (24%) with salesmen

8 days (3%) with sales supervisors

111 days (45%) in the office

It is significant that the manager spent so much less time with his supervisors than with the account managers and salesmen. The manager's logic is evident: he wanted to control key account volume, have first-hand knowledge about developments in the trade, and learn the retailer's reactions to proposed promotions. Obviously, the manager assumed that his supervisors were competent (which confidence, in reality, was justified).

His office time was spread over a number of activities which were hard to separate. He spent many hours in informal discussions with any of the salesmen who "dropped by." These discussions might solicit opinions on future strategy, trade developments, competitive programs, or any other problem currently on the manager's desk. Sometimes, the sessions were for counseling purposes. Whatever their format, the informal meetings were the manager's major technique for communicating and for giving the salesmen a sense of participation in district affairs.

As a supplement to these informal contacts, the manager expected regular telephone calls from the team concerning competitive activities. A complete flow of intelligence was critical to the manager. He used these data for recommending special promotional programs for the district. The cornerstone of his personal policy was to gain more than his share of the company's promotional funds—an objective which required detailed knowledge of competitive action, as well as programs for offsetting the action. It follows that our manager was in touch with his superior (the area manager) 3 or 4 times each week. Most often, these contacts were by phone but sometimes in the form of handwritten notes. The purpose, however, was always the same: to gain support for the branch's programs.

Although the manager relied primarily upon informal channels of communication, he did write a weekly bulletin for the salesmen. Additionally, he held monthly planning sessions with his supervisors and account managers.

The manager spent a significant part of his time on such organizational matters as a review of the branch's territory coverage plan, development programs for individual men, and a continuous evaluation of sales performance. Occasional special reports were prepared for the home office, and much personal interaction took place with the warehouse manager concerning local supply and shipping problems. The manager gave no time to trade association activities, a characteristic not shared by his predecessor.

Sentiments Much can be learned about the branch manager by considering his attitudes or sentiments. In brief, he defined his mission as building the Andrews franchise through continuous competitive analyses; aggressive, "no-holds-barred" selling; and personal control over key account volume. He stressed the need for team effort and for each salesman to act as if he were "sales manager" for his accounts. In the manager's words: "Selling is easy. The real job is to see that the product moves through the store to the housewife. This requires intensive in-store work, merchandising ideas, and attention to the retailer's problems." The manager, moreover, was steadfast in his conviction that the "name of the game" was to "clobber" competition—that anything he could do to gain the upper hand was desirable. This dedication to victory meant that, in many respects, the manager believed that the end justified the means.

So much for a general summary of the manager's attitudes. Some selected quotations make the specifics clearer.

1. *Attitudes about his job.* He had a direct-action philosophy.

> My job is to produce sales. I don't care how.
> I'll act today and worry about the problems tomorrow.

He could verbalize a basic selling strategy clearly.

> You build a franchise by selling features, which requires a dollar advantage and control of the shelves. You control shelves because competition is lax in this regard, and shelf position enhances features since the housewife typically goes first to the shelf.

He had a clear understanding of the need for open communication.

> A two-way flow of information is essential so the salesmen can manage their accounts and so that I can argue for the proper deals and promotions. I always tell the men in advance about pending deals. This means that we can activate any promotion the first day because the salesmen have known how to treat their accounts during the previous two weeks.

He was self-sufficient. He argued, for example, that the branch manager should make his own decisions, that local problems should be solved on the spot.

> Don't ask for help unless you also have a solution.

He was flexible and ingenious. In these respects, he rarely tackled an argument head-on if he could "get around" the resistance by some alternative course.

He was "people-oriented." He made himself freely available to the salesmen on the basis that:

> Salesmen need confidence. You develop this by demonstrating *how* when a man is finally stuck. I try to inspire my team, to set an example and not push them too directly.

He was ready to go with them personally on any tough call.

He was dedicated to his job. In all conversations, this manager was constantly intrigued with matters of business. He was forever probing for new ideas, inquiring, seeking alternatives, "thinking aloud" about better strategy and how to lick competition.

He believed that a manager must be positive, optimistic, energetic, self-confident, and more competent than the men whom he supervised.

He believed in direct intervention on major accounts. Although the manager never visited a major customer without the account manager, he felt that his title and personal skills were legitimate weapons for gaining key customer support.

2. *Attitudes about the sales group.* He was convinced that the secret to success was to hire aggressive, intelligent people and force their growth with early responsibility. Each sales person was treated as an individual and motivated on a personal basis.

> Prove to me by your (the noncollege salesman) sales performance that I can recommend you for the special program at Michigan State. Prove to me that I should recommend you (the man who came from an advertising background) for product management.

Each man was respected for his ideas and knowledge. For example, the salesmen were openly invited to suggest strategic moves, to assess branch progress and needs, and to volunteer any other ideas relevant to the operations.

His standards were explicit:

> Our job is to sell. Selling is easy. Either you sell or you get out. I'm here to help you sell.

Each salesman, in this respect, was expected to gain a competitive edge in his accounts by aggression, service, imaginative selling, displays, shelf control, and post-sale merchandising. He did not tolerate mediocre performance and was quick to put anyone "on warning" who was not working up to his abilities.

He relied heavily upon "bonus earnings" as a continuing spur to the salesmen.

> I remind them that every sale they lose is bread out of their mouths. They are all excited about these large bonus checks.

He expected each to be business-oriented and to manage the accounts without constant supervision.

3. *Attitudes about competition.* It has already been stated that the branch manager had strong feelings about competition. As he said:

> Competition is the enemy. We give no quarter nor expect any. I train my men to demoralize competition, to beat them off the shelf, to spread rumors about them, to keep them off balance and on the run.

The intensity of the manager's feelings was evident in much of his behavior. He warned his salesforce, for example, to avoid personal contacts with competitors. He followed the same rule. He had no patience with arguments that the competitors were better and, in fact, was convinced that Andrews Food would put them all to rout.

One could almost conclude that the branch manager was less concerned with meeting the needs of his customers than he was with beating the competition. The at least partial truth of this statement will be discussed later.

4. *Attitudes about selling.* We have seen that our manager looked upon increasing sales as his key responsibility. Selling, therefore, was the pivot of the manager's world. He had strong feelings about it. To be specific, he believed that selling was easy and fun. It was, moreover, the key ingredient to building a franchise. The manager knew that competitive deals were essential, but their specifics—the way in which they were presented, the competitive edge in the separate stores, the strategies for gaining trade support—were all dependent upon personal effort. Strong selling makes the deals work—that was the branch's chief point of view.

Selling was considered as more than gaining the large orders. The team was reminded often that:

> You can always make sales if you have a plan to move the merchandise out of the store.

To repeat, the men were expected to move the merchandise *in* and *through* the stores.

The inevitable consequence of this selling orientation was that the manager also assumed sales responsibilities, although on an indirect basis. He kept an eye on the major customers. In fact, when he took over the poor branch, his early emphasis was upon plans and presentations for capturing key volume. This personal control was another important aspect of the strong manager's behavior.

5. *Attitudes about company policy.* Because the district manager was dedicated to results, fast action, and local autonomy, it is no surprise to learn that he took a liberal view of company policies. By his standards, policy was a *general* guide, not an operational dictum. Policy required local interpretation due to competition and other pressures. "Wheeling and dealing" were justifiable if they increased market share and if "you get your money's worth from the retailer every time you stretch the rules." Moreover, this manager's dedication to his

company and product meant that he saw his behavior as "best for the company."

Interrelationships The third aspect of management behavior has to do with personal interaction and with the role assumed by the manager during these interrelationships. By way of summary, a number of things can be said about our manager. In the first place, he was a man who *listened,* who went out of his way to seek alternatives and new ideas. Secondly, he was an effective communications link between the field salesmen and the home office. He "translated" home office directives into the language of his men and correspondingly translated field requests into home office language. Between himself and his sales group, he ensured open communications. He was as frank with them as he expected them to be with him. Thirdly, the manager "put himself on the line." He never hesitated to intercede on behalf of his colleagues and considered such intercession a prime responsibility. Let us examine the nature of the manager's interpersonal behavior more specifically.

1. *Relationship with his staff.* We saw earlier that the manager concentrated his attention upon the accounts managers, and we know why. What was the nature of this relationship?

The branch manager played the role of peer when discussing key account strategy with specific individuals. Thus, the two would exchange thoughts and information about the characteristics of the account, the idiosyncrasies of the buyers, and the details of a proposed strategy.

But the manager became "the expert" when making a joint call upon a key buyer. The two normally planned the part of the presentation that each would make. The manager's major emphasis was upon the basic message: "We are here to show you how to sell three times as much Andrews," but he carefully left the impression that the salesman was responsible for the account. "I will back 100 percent any commitments the accounts manager makes to you."

Once the account was under control, the branch manager left most of the selling to the account manager. During this stage, his role was that of adviser.

The staff (account managers and sales supervisors) was the manager's prime agency for recommending strategy, promotions, and customer tactics. He met with the group formally twice each month in so-called "planning" meetings. But he met with the four informally more often. Whenever they passed the office, he would invite their suggestions. His role was again as fellow discussant. But he was all business and rarely allowed the discussions to drift into generalizations or social discourses.

Needless to say, he took the staff fully into his confidence (such as revealing the pending deals) and implicitly assumed that they would treat the knowledge with discretion.

2. *Relationships with the salesmen.* The intriguing aspect of the manager's relationship with his men was how he could seemingly treat them as peers, maintain an informal relationship with each, and yet protect his position as supervisor. To each of the salesmen, the manager was equally available, and from each, he sought advice and suggestions. He kept them all informed about future deals and correspondingly expected them to keep him informed about competition. The benefits of this open rapport warrant repetition. The manager was assured of the evidence about competition he needed to obtain promotional funds from company headquarters, and the men felt that they were important contributors to branch operations.

Because the salesmen knew that their manager would personally intercede whenever they had trouble, they had little hesitation about "going along" with the manager's plans. As one new man said, "Because of the manager's support, I soon learned that there's no reason to fear retailer reactions. All they can do is yell at you."

Perhaps the best way to sum up this aspect of the manager's behavior is to say that he was a superb supervisor. He was able to lead and inspire his men.

3. *Relations with the home office.* Just as the manager worked at keeping the channels free between himself and his men, he worked hard at maintaining a two-way flow between himself and the area manager. He most often used the telephone but did not neglect written and personal contacts. Commonly, he initiated the contact. Most of the interchange concerned competition and recommendations for promotional programs. Additionally, the manager kept the home office fully informed about any noteworthy achievements by the salesmen.

The manager, it must be noted, did not pass along all of his problems to higher management. If it could be solved locally, that was always the manager's first choice. For example, there were some differences of opinion between the branch and the warehouse manager. Rather than appeal for top management intervention, the branch manager worked out acceptable compromises with the warehouse manager which were then passed up the line for approval. This was a distinguishing characteristic of the manager. He rarely asked for assistance until he had a solution firmly in mind. In his words: "I try not to ask for action until I've got my ducks lined up."

4. *Relation with key buyers.* We have already seen that a major aspect of the manager's behavior was personal involvement in key accounts. This was how he attempted to build a franchise and ensure quota attainment. There is no need to repeat the data already presented regarding the manager's role in these relationships. Suffice it to say that his great personal selling skill was used to advantage and his contribution was supplementary to that of the account manager's.

Decisions Our man was decisive. He was action-oriented and believed that some activity was better than none. Some of his decisions can be neatly categorized. For example, many were intended to change the status quo whenever the environment operated to the manager's disadvantage. Others were intended to create excitement in the trade and to keep competition off balance. Rarely, we know, did he worry about the precision of company policies. His objective was to get results, and, in this regard, his behavior was single-minded.

The manager would adopt any reasonable action which produced sales or provided a competitive edge. He believed that his abilities could overcome the problems any precipitate action created. When he sold to an anticipated deal, as in one case, and the ensuing terms were less advantageous to the retailer than promised, he and his men managed to calm most of the buyers personally. His later rationalization was that the early promises to the trade resulted in major volume gains which more than offset the resulting customer complaints (which were not, in reality, too numerous).

A vital part of the manager's "deal policy" was the use of display allowances. He used these to ensure in-store movement, to "sweeten the pot," and to give Andrews a public reputation of being "on the move."

Some of his major decisions related to steps for gaining momentum by cracking important accounts. Such early successes were used as testimonials for persuading other reluctant retailers.

The manager made equally important decisions among the wholesale accounts. He wanted their support in order to counterbalance the direct selling advantages of his competitors. Moreover, by working through wholesalers, he was able to pyramid deals into longer-time periods.

He also tried to do "dramatic" things in order to pull away from his competition. He pushed to be the sponsor of the local professional team, to introduce 5-pound sizes, to execute "Operation Pitchout" (convincing the retailer that he should drop slowly moving competitive lines), and to "blitz" the smaller stores periodically with a task force of salesmen.

This manager was equally decisive about manpower. He would not tolerate below-par performers. He initiated local incentive programs to reward men for obtaining competitive intelligence, and he instituted indirect sales budgets in order to encourage their missionary efforts among wholesalers.

SUMMARY AND CONCLUDING REMARKS

We have explored several issues pertinent to sales management. What are our major conclusions? What advice do we have for the neophyte sales manager?

1. Establish selling goals and objectives and make it clear to all what the sales department's mission is. Where are we trying to go? What is our role in the overall strategy? What kinds of sales do we want?

2. Communicate by your words and action the company's pride in its sales force. Give deserved recognition, but at the same time make it clear that you won't tolerate slipshod performance. In this regard, many managers find that published rankings of the salespeople spur remedial action by the laggards.

3. Be sure of the fundamentals—the job requirements, the market and customers, the products, the service and back-up support, the competitors. More exactly, the sales organization should excel in the critical selling area, be it demonstration, application know-how, service support, missionary calls, or prospecting. Even though the sales managers won't "do," they must understand the job requirements in order to coach and evaluate performance.

4. Use a sensible control system of call reports, working plans, forecasts, and quotas—if you don't use the data, don't ask for them!

5. Solicit inputs from the field organization. Not only are their ideas usually sensible, but the local individuals want the excitement of knowing that their suggestions are considered.

6. Don't ignore the details. They often unlock the toughest puzzles. Like football coaches, it's a good idea for the sales manager to debrief the sales team after important wins or losses. Call a special

Monday-morning review of why a deal was lost: do not accept less than an open discussion of the real reasons behind the loss.

7. Compensate for the team's weakness by shifting the defense or offense to cover weakness or exploit strength. The effective sales manager may be at a competitive disadvantage because of price, product limitations, or slow delivery. Nevertheless he capitalizes on his particular assets and designs a different customer strategy. He or she asks, "What is my competitor's edge and how can I neutralize it?" Hence the importance of firsthand observations— making calls and finding out what is going on.

8. Hold an endless series of informative, positive meetings with all those involved in the sales process, including dealers and reps.

9. Make sure that you and your team know the facts about sales and profits: Which accounts, industries, geographies are the key ones? How much profit does each contribute? What is the profitability of each rep?

10. Make educational and development programs available to the entire sales force. It's easy to forget that successful performers "give" constantly of themselves. How do they get the chance to renew their intellectual and emotional batteries?

11. Instill enthusiasm. Communicate the fact that selling is an exciting, fun game. System and purpose may be a necessary foundation, but the spirit and excitement of the chase is the satisfying individual payoff.

10

The Last Word

For the emerging company, marketing is typically the critical function. So often the new enterprise springs from the product idea of an entrepreneur. The invention is the focus: can we build it? will it work? can we make it fast enough? where can we get the money?

These are the normal initial problems for the start-up firm. It's not that marketing is ignored—rather that the cleverness of the invention reinforces the technical bias and the underlying faith that "of course they will buy it!"

In the course of new company development, the early focus upon product and technology is understandable. Not many such enterprises start with an analysis of customer needs and then invent to order. Indeed, such a utopian approach would be expensive and time consuming. Which users should I think about? Which of their needs should I select? The search process, assuming no other resource than the desire to "start a company," is almost without bounds.

The fact is that most new company ideas evolve out of an existing operation. The products or the customers suggest a specific starting point. "Why can't I re-engineer the power station to allow . . . etc." Or, "Customer Jones wants to know if we can solve his particular problem with condensation leakage."

So off we go with an improved product based in part, at least, on some prior technology. The entrepreneur's key preoccupation is with "the invention." The challenge is to make it. And it must be noted that many companies get a nice launch by springboarding from such an engineering base.

But consider the risks—the bad things that could happen.

1. The product has limited application.

2. The product is only marginally superior to its competition.

3. The wrong buyers are targeted, leaving the prime market to some competitor.

4. The product is over-engineered.

5. Or, the product is designed to be "all things to all people."

6. A new technology wipes it out.

7. The price is set too low to finance future growth.

8. The distribution strategy is poorly executed, distributors are mediocre and the inadequate sales force makes fewer sales than anticipated.

9. The firm establishes a customer image of "great technology, no application or service."

10. A new product is introduced for future delivery—and present sales dry up.

11. Service is essentially ignored.

12. R & D concentrates on the newest facets of the technology—not the utility.

We could go on, forever, with our little horror list. There are an incredible number of bear traps that the emerging enterprise can step into. They are not, of course, all marketing-derived. But many of them are.

For the growing firm, therefore, marketing represents the opportunity to launch in a more reasonable manner. In particular, a successful marketing input establishes early direction for the firm, identifies appropriate markets and products, and creates a strategy which supplies a boost in the marketplace.

The new company cannot start this marketing thrust too early. The canny entrepreneur, assuming he is not the marketing specialist, will latch onto a marketing professional as his first hire—a choice more important than getting the money man, the manufacturing specialist or the second engineer. Without the marketing skill there is no meaningful focus for constructing the rest of the company. As long as the customer remains the critical success variable, there is no other viable alternative.

Marketing, then, is more than a perfunctory function for the new firm. It is the driving force behind business definition and direction, competitive strategy (or how to win in the jungle), and making the sale.

Index